The Forbidden Male Speaks

Messages from Jeshua on love, relationships, and heart-based masculinity

Pamela Kribbe

BookLocker
Trenton, Georgia

Print ISBN: 978-1-958891-85-8
Ebook ISBN: 979-8-88531-663-7

Published by BookLocker.com, Inc., Trenton, Georgia.

BookLocker.com, Inc.

2024

First Edition

Translation by Pamela Kribbe and Suzy Conway from Dutch

Content

Introduction

The purpose of this book is to acquaint you with the energy of the forbidden male and allow him room to speak. Who is this forbidden male and is there a forbidden male hidden in all of us?

Our culture is characterized by male dominance in all aspects of our lives; social, political, religious, and family. For centuries, the king, the priest, the judge, and the head of the family were positions reserved for men. Throughout our patriarchal history, it is men who have privilege. So how does it follow that they were denied anything? Don't we usually think it is the women who are oppressed and forbidden to express and develop themselves?

In the last century, the modern woman has enjoyed increasing emancipation. She has fought for her rights and made progress, has more say in all areas of her life, and yet, she is often angry at men. They were and still are the perpetrators and oppressors who continue to curtail her. But through experience, and over time, she has learned to manage them more effectively. In modern days, the male is not necessarily the leader and head of the family, and he is increasingly portrayed as authoritarian, callous, macho, and often emotionally absent.

This traditional man not only withholds women's rights, but is usually too absorbed in his work, lacks proper communication skills, is emotionally unavailable, often regards women as sex objects, and understands nothing about spirituality. This side that is so evident in men is presently under fierce scrutiny. But does this image match how they truly feel and think? What do we really object to when we judge them? Is it something inherent in them or is it the image of masculinity that men may feel stuck with and are obligated to conform to? That is an important question, because when we speak of an image, we are dealing with a human construction.

An image is created from our own expectations, wishes and ideals, and is more often a distortion than a true reflection of reality. In other words, is our image of masculinity a true reflection of how men really are or is it a distortion or a perversion? Thus, the bigger question is what constitutes true manhood?

While a lot of emphasis is put on the importance of women's emancipation and a broader understanding of what femininity is, it is assumed that we understand what masculinity is, but is it obvious? Is the masculine energy really competitive, combative, decisive, controlling, emotionally absent, and sex-hungry? Or are men stuck with this caricature? Is it an image they have to live up to in order to survive socially and emotionally? If this is the case, then what is the price they pay for it? What happens when someone is forced into a straitjacket construed of images and expectations that do not fit them, but is so ubiquitous and heavy they cannot and dare not break out? What emotional wounds does this cause? What goes underground and becomes forbidden in the male psyche because of the pervasive influence of this traditional image, and how does it affect men, their relationships, and the world at large?

There is a blind spot in our present-day awareness about what constitutes masculinity which will be a point of discussion in this book. It is a topic that is rarely explored, or it is explored superficially and does not begin to address what I call "the male wound." The violent nature men can exhibit is embedded in the age-old image of masculinity that we have collectively inherited and its disruptive effect on boys and men will also be discussed.

The forbidden male who tried to emerge was driven underground because his originality, sensitivity and truth-telling were not tolerated by the existing rules, expectations, and ideals around acceptable male behavior.

The need for men to go underground leads to a host of psychological problems. On the collective level, it leads to loneliness, emotional repression, impoverished relationships, aggression, violence and a lack of creativity and inspiration. Men suffer from an imposed image of masculinity, which has far reaching consequences. It has a profound effect not only on their psyches, but also on their relationships with women, other men, their sons, daughters and ultimately has profound consequences on a global scale. The world is still dominated on the international political level by a form of male leadership based on an impoverished and dehumanized image of masculinity.

It is time to understand the destructive consequences that are wrought on men who are trying to live up to this image. I will shed light on how to break out of this straight jacket on an inner level and to arrive at a new understanding of masculinity. It is about time this forbidden man speaks out.

The forbidden male was and still is the original face of manhood. It is the masculine aspect of the soul representing clarity, insight, innovation, and creativity. This loving male energy wants to protect life. As an aspect of the soul, the forbidden male is present in both women and men, for the soul encompasses both the masculine and the feminine. The original masculine energy within us helps bring a unique individuality to the fore which needs to express itself in this earthly reality.

The forbidden male is not just a man, per se, but an energy that is valuable for everyone to rediscover and awaken within themselves, women as well as men. We are on Earth to express our unique soul and the integration of our original masculine and feminine sides is fundamental to this.

The original power of the masculine energy—naturally inquisitive, free, and adventurous has been severely suppressed, distorted and wounded. We know that women have been victims of a paternalistic tradition; however, this applies to men too. Their psyches and self-image have been profoundly damaged by an aggressive and inhuman ideal of "how a man should be." This has had such an overwhelming influence on all of us that we have come to accept that men are "simply that way".

In 2018, I wrote *The Forbidden Female Speaks,* which highlights how women have been psychologically and emotionally wounded throughout history and how they still struggle despite the gains for equal rights and increased opportunities for their personal and social development. Their wound is a persistent feeling of unworthiness, the tendency to give and care too much, and the inability to fully assume one's own autonomy. The liberation of the forbidden male does not only apply to men.

In this book, I make a crucial point—women do not dare embrace their own masculine energy. It is true that they have learned how to behave "manly" in the workplace, but that kind of energy is in fact the traditional, handed down, tough and competitive kind which does not represent authentic masculine energy at all. I will explain that women also need to excavate the original masculine energy within and awaken "the forbidden male" which holds as deep a meaning for them as for men.

It is important for women to regain their autonomous soul power by making positive contact with their own masculine energy. This empowers them to become mature creators, release patterns of over-giving, and dependence, and be more open to equal-partner relationships. The "forbidden masculine energy" is one of autonomy, self-respect, and vision.

The traditional masculine energy is at odds with the feminine because it depicts it as weak, capricious, and emotional. However, the mature, primordial, masculine energy is in natural harmony with the feminine qualities of connection, empathy, and intuition.

The distorted images that have come down to us about masculinity and femininity strongly influence our relationships and our perspective on love. This book addresses our desires and expectations about relationships and intimacy.

The idea of "the forbidden male" is relevant here as well. In their relationships with men, women are still taken in, often half-consciously, by stereotypical images of masculinity that enormously confound them. They have ambiguous expectations of men. In their romantic dreams, they still expect the arrival of the knight in shining armor, the tower of strength, the powerful leader and protector. Subconsciously, they still associate masculinity with being tough, strong, and unyielding. But in practice, they crave meaningful communication, emotional intimacy, and a deep human connection. These expectations are at odds with each other. Men have comparable ambiguous expectations—a mix of stereotypical and ideal images on the one hand and a desire for authentic connection on the other.

Behind the constructed images of the masculine and feminine by which we define ourselves lies the reality of our unique individuality. Within all of us, male or female, there lives a spark of individuality and originality that emanates from our souls. We are not bodies, but souls, inspired beings that live in a male or female body. The soul contains both aspects, possesses both masculine and feminine energy. These two poles are an essential part of everything that exists in all of creation.

The root of many problems becomes apparent when we disregard this and identify too strongly with being male or female. This is tantamount to denying or suppressing one's unique individuality as a soul. Relationships that are not based on soul contact are rife with expectations and archetypal images about man and womanhood, but they lack soulful masculinity and femininity. Beyond stereotypical images of the ideal man or woman lies the unfathomable depth of the human soul.

The forbidden male energy is of interest to all of us. In spiritual circles now there is often talk of the rebirth of the feminine energy at this time. However, there is an equally urgent need for the rebirth of masculine energy. The face of the original male energy has been hidden for too long in the existing order with disastrous consequences for the well-being of man and nature.

This book pleads for a return to soulful masculinity—breaking the taboo on heart-based masculine energy, acknowledging the emotional wounding in men by awakening women to embrace their own masculine energy and, finally, by freeing both men and women from compulsive desires and stereotypes. Then, once more, there will be space for the soul to participate in relationships. Imagine a battlefield where the soul returns to bring healing.

What is channeling?

This book consists of channeled information. What you find on the pages is information intuitively received from sources that lie beyond the material earthly plane. Traditionally, the word "mediumship" is used for this mode of communication. From my perspective, channeling is a form of collaboration between a spiritual source and an earthly human being. This source is at the level of our soul. The teacher or energy being channeled is part of a reality beyond space, time, and matter. This reality is not outside of us, but present within us, and accessible through our heart and intuition.

To clarify how channeling works, I will go back to 2002, to explain how it all began. I started my aura reading practice that year. My partner Gerrit and I both had a profound interest in philosophy and spirituality throughout our lives. I earned a PhD in philosophy, while Gerrit worked as a computer scientist and had a thorough knowledge of hypnotherapy, astrology, and esoteric literature.

When we moved in together in 2001, we made it a practice to conduct sessions in the evening where I went into a trance state. With his wide range of experience and affinity with hypnotherapy, Gerrit guided me along as we explored many aspects of our psychological makeup—emotional blocks, past lives, and broad questions about life and spirituality.

One night during a session, I felt a presence I didn't recognize. I had previously interacted with guides and spiritual teachers who surrounded me with gentle energy and loving suggestions, but this was different. This presence felt serious and penetrating. We decided to investigate who or what it was, and when I connected with this energy, it felt like a wise, masculine presence. I very clearly saw the name "Jeshua ben Joseph" appear before my inner eye, the Aramaic name for Jesus.

In the flash of a second, deep down, I knew it was true. I had felt the energy of Jesus. At the same time, a chorus of skeptical, rational voices started singing in my head, telling me that it could not be true, that it was weird, ridiculous, and pretentious. This choir has never been completely silenced, but it does sing a bit softer now.

We have had so many wonderful and valuable experiences and encounters in our lives after connecting with Jeshua and the Christ energy that I was gradually convinced that there is indeed something there and that it does not only come from me.

Right after meeting Jeshua, I could feel him with me. He helped me during individual aura consultations to stay grounded, thus protecting myself from becoming too over-stimulated because sometimes, I would feel energetically exhausted after a reading. Jeshua taught me how to strengthen and maintain my boundaries. (Masculine energy!) He did this through an energy transfer and through short, telepathic messages.

I always feel centered when I tune in to Jeshua's energy. It's a matter of becoming quiet and focused, and letting go of irrelevant worrisome thoughts and emotions. It is a feeling of inner freedom.

During this first phase of our collaborations with Jeshua we did not confide in or tell anyone what was happening until well over a year. Then, we told some good friends about what was unfolding and organized small sessions with them. Gerrit and I received a series of messages from Jeshua (later published in the book *The Jeshua Channelings*) and we made them available on the internet.

In April 2004, we were invited to a spiritual center in Belgium to do a channeling in front of a live audience. I felt I must accept this invitation even though I had some mighty fears to overcome. This meeting was the start of many channeled lectures that were held in the presence of increasingly larger groups of people. I had to contend with my fears and reservations around channeling when we went public in this way.

And yet, the atmosphere in the meetings was so special and the energy of Jeshua so palpable that I was inspired to continue. We met many people at these meetings and later in the workshops we offered. We felt a natural like-mindedness with them, shared common interests, and an openness to the spiritual. Jeshua's energy paved the way for me to encounter my "spiritual family" through short-lived encounters. These interactions were very important, some even became long-lasting friendships. All were precious gifts.

What happens during channeling? This is a question I do not have a definitive answer to, but I can describe how it feels. I was already familiar with the trance state from my work as an aura reader before I started channeling. Trance consciousness takes a combination of being relaxed and alert. In the trance state, my body feels more fluid, lighter, and I can look at an issue freely and openly without thinking too much about it.

In the trance state you perceive intuitively. It is a "knowing feeling", not charged with emotion or judgment. This does not mean that you perceive everything correctly, however. The degree to which you clearly and strongly perceive depends on the emotional balance you have achieved within. It's never perfect, but the more you grow inwardly, the easier you can observe things openly and freely. I am convinced that in developing skills such as aura reading and channeling, one's own personal inner development becomes much more important than learning certain techniques.

In the trance state, for me at least, I never feel a loss of control. I have never lost consciousness during a trance state, nor have I ever lost consciousness when channeling Jeshua. It would be more accurate to say that my self-awareness is heightened as Jeshua's energy and messages flow through me. I don't feel switched off, but I do feel switched on at a deeper level within myself, a level that I cannot easily reach in my everyday life.

When I channel, I am aware of who I really am. My higher self or the angelic being that I actually am is revealed to me. When I am channeling, you could say that my "little self" connects with my "higher self" and Jeshua's energy mediates this. It seems like his energy enables me to genuinely feel and accept my own greatness.

When people experience the phenomenon of channeling, the danger that can arise is that they regard the knowledge or message that comes through as by definition higher or better because it comes from "the beyond". But this is not the case. The true test of any channeled information is the clarity and love that is expressed throughout it. Who or what is being channeled is of secondary importance.

It is also important to know that channeled messages are colored by the individual experience and understanding of the one who conveys them. The purity of the channeling is not determined by the channeler switching themselves off completely, (that is impossible) but by their ability to serve the energy that is being channeled. They do not distort it, or they distort it as little as possible, while being aware of their own judgments and fears. The crucial question one should ask about any spiritual message is does it come from love or from fear? This is the more important question to ask rather than who the author of the message is.

Remember, the last thing a true spiritual teacher wants is for you to accept what they tell you because they say so. A request for such submission to authority goes against the essence of spirituality. All you really need to know lies within yourself. There is no authority outside of you, no "ascended master" or "being of light" that knows better.

In the philosophy of science, the branch of philosophy that deals with the question "What is science?", there is a school of thought that purports that our everyday ideas are subjective, and that science (physics) holds the objective truth about reality. You could call this objectivism.

Other contemporary philosophers argue that scientific ideas are strongly influenced by unproven, historically determined assumptions and subjective expectations. They believe that science shows only one interpretation of the world, one version of the truth. You could call this relativism, the stance that there is no point of view that is completely objective, in the sense that it is independent of any (subjective) observer. I myself am inclined to subscribe to relativism and I think it is pertinent to channeling and mediumship, as well.

Sometimes people expect that speaking with "the other world" puts them in touch with the objective truth, the revelation of how things really are free of the human perspective. This is a mistake. Perspectives from the other side remain perspectives. They should be enlightening, inspiring and give you hope, strength and courage, but they don't necessarily reveal the ultimate truth. Remember they are channeled by human beings who are heavily influenced by their cultural background, for one, and that's okay, however, the idea that there is an ultimate truth—in the sense that there is one objectively correct worldview or system of thought has not served us well in the past.

I do believe there is such a thing as an energy of truth. This is an energy that emanates from loving, authentic people. You may feel it when you are moved by a beautiful work of art, or when you're out in the wilds of nature. It is an energy of clarity and simplicity. In that energy, we sense something we may try to capture in words, ideas, or theories, but it eludes us, because it can never be reduced to words and concepts.

Jeshua's channelings contain this energy of truth but do not tell you how it really is. They do tell you that the truth can be found within you. In other words, the channelings do not so much tell the truth, as make the "energy of the truth" tangible. If you feel this energy when reading Jeshua's messages, then the purpose of this book has been achieved.

Below are some words from Jeshua himself about the phenomenon of channeling. So what follows is a channeling about channeling.

Channeling is a way to get closer to yourself through another. This "other" temporarily fulfills the function of a teacher, and their energy helps you to not only go to a deeper level within yourself but also lifts you out of the fear that hides your essential light. A teacher sees your light better than you see it and shows you your own light. Once this light becomes visible and accessible to you, the teacher becomes superfluous. At this point, you can start to channel your own light. The other no longer has to be the bridge between you and your higher self.

I will remind you of your own light, for a while. I reflect your greatness to you in the form of Jeshua ben Joseph. You see yourself in me, your Christ self, but you do not know this yet. I am your frame of reference; my energy is a guideline for you. I help you connect more deeply with your own Christ self. When it gradually comes to the fore, then I move to the background. This is good. Remember, in this relationship, I am here for you, you are not here for me. I am not an end, but a means. The rebirth of the Christ energy is the resurrection of your Christ self, not mine.

I do what promotes your greatness. My goal is for you to make me obsolete. When you channel me, don't make yourself small or invisible. I want you to make yourself bigger, feel your true power flowing and let your light shine in the world.

A teacher shows the way, but you walk it. After a while you notice that you are walking alone and have left the teacher behind. This is a great and sacred moment. The teacher remains with you, and dwells in your heart as an inner form, but his outer form disappears.

We remain connected, but in time you will recognize me less and less as a separate figure and want to summon me. I have then become your own energy. You no longer know me as separate from you. This means that you really heard me and saw me.

The structure of the book

Part I of this book includes messages from Jeshua about masculinity and the transition of consciousness from ego to heart. The importance of masculine heart energy is explained first on a fundamental metaphysical level. The masculine energy creates separation and helps the soul move out of Oneness so it can go its individual way. In addition, Jeshua explains the value of the heart-based male energy which concerns sensitivity and boundaries. The more sensitive and open your consciousness becomes in the transition from ego to heart, the more important it becomes to use your own masculine energy to create space for yourself and connect with your soul. The channelings in this section also include a number of guided meditations that energetically connect you with your own masculine heart energy.

In part II, I ask Jeshua questions about male and female energy. In this dialogue with him, the wound in the male energy is described in depth as a wound of the heart that has cut men off from their souls. It is important that men recognize this wound and rethink their definition of masculinity. When there is room for a different image of masculine energy, in which the heart plays a prominent role, it creates healing not only in men, but in women, in partnerships and in society as a whole. Specifically, the effect of masculine heart energy in relationships is discussed, how it creates space for a free, mature connection that honors the individuality of the other and in which illusions about unity and "melting into oneness" are released.

Finally, in part III, there are four meditations that will help you contact your original masculine heart energy. These channeled meditations came through during a workshop for men but are equally valuable for women. Not only is it important for women to understand the collective wound in men, but it is also essential that they connect with their own masculine energy.

Part I- Messages from Jeshua

Chapter 1- The separation of the sexes

In this channeling, Jeshua discusses how a soul is born and evolves into an individual being. Besides being "cast out" from the Oneness, the soul undergoes a second moment of separation when a split occurs between male and female. The soul chooses to take a male or female form on its path of incarnation and this separation or limitation has both a painful and a creative aspect to it. Jeshua explains how separateness reflects the masculine aspect of creation, and how this allows for depth and creativity. What we are growing towards on our path of consciousness is an inner balance between connection and self-awareness, between unity (feminine) and separateness (masculine).

I am Jeshua. I welcome you. You are dear to me.

I wish to tell you of an old pain that lies dormant in your consciousness. Many of your daily emotional difficulties, and the turmoil that is within you, stem from a primal psychic pain that I call "the pain of separation." There is a wound in you, an emptiness that you keep trying to fill. In most of you, this primal pain is often unconscious yet present in the background. Because you are not aware of the origin of this pain, you try to solve it by achieving outer goals—the inspiring job that suits you, the ultimate lover, or the right lifestyle.

If these remain out of reach, you feel unhappy, unfulfilled, and doubt the meaning of your existence. But the real cause of your pain is not attaining your outer goal, it lies on a much deeper level—the primal pain and wound of separation.

I want to speak about the cause or origin of this existential void. "Emptiness" when used here is another word for "separation". You experienced your first separation at the beginning of your journey as a soul when you were separating from the Whole or Unity. Mind you, when I speak of the soul and how it began or was birthed in time, we are actually crossing the border of what can be understood by the human mind. So don't take my words too literally for in this story I'm going to tell you, I use images to make tangible how you came into being.

Imagine that in those distant beginnings there existed a primordial water, a vast sea surrounded by the expanse of heaven. The celestial space in which the water is located represents consciousness. Space itself is nothing, at least not in the material sense. It is pure consciousness. The water represents life, movement, dynamics and feeling. There was a time when you were in that water.

Imagine you are part of the water moving with the current. You might feel your boundaries slowly dissolving. You melt into the water; it feels soft and pleasantly cool. If you vividly imagine yourself absorbed in that primordial water, you may feel that you no longer have a body. Your body has dissolved and all you are now is a point of consciousness. You are one with the water and do not experience the limitations of having a body. You feel that the water surrounds you, and at the same time you are the water. It is a strange sensation.

Feel how in that diffuse self that you are, there arises a desire for air to breathe. This desire suddenly makes you focus. You identify with that need and your awareness becomes fixed on that one goal—air and breathing. You've never breathed before, but something inside you knows you want to experience this and this something pulls and pushes you to the surface of the water. Suddenly you raise your head from this womb-like sea and take a breath. You are incarnated! You are in physical form. You are a body that breathes.

Feel that first, deep breath and become aware of your physicality. The longing for the breath of life has made you a corporeal being. No longer are you absorbed in the water, in the oceanic unity. You are now separate, independent, and autonomous and what has brought you into that separation is the fire of your desire. This desire that arises from the masculine aspect of your consciousness as a soul is a creative desire. It wants to break free from the oneness because it has a deep and passionate desire to experience life. The longing for selfhood, incarnation and separateness is a creative desire, because only through the self, through subjective feeling, does the experience of life become your experience.

This feeling is subjective. You feel things in your individual way which is not possible within the safety of the primordial sea. Because of separation, a limited self and a subjective consciousness arise, along with duality and diversity. There are many incarnated conscious sparks who have their own perspective and their own experience, and this diversity brings problems along with it, a sense of fragmentation, and a sense of being in opposition to other individual souls, at times.

In the primeval sea you were one, and in that sense safe and secure. When you were ushered out of this oceanic womb it was painful and confusing because for the first time, you felt disconnected. When you become an individual and are separated from the whole, it is a leap of faith for the soul, an adventure that beckons and at the same time disconcerts. This jump into duality comes from the creative fire in the soul itself, but at the same time it produces deep confusion—the primal pain of being cast out of oneness.

You can compare that metaphysical primal pain with what happens when a little baby exits the womb and is born on earth. It leaves its safe environment and experiences the difference between itself and the outside world. The passage from unity to separateness repeats itself with each incarnation. Every time the soul takes the leap into the earthly domain, and breathes in duality and diversity, it leaves the oneness to take on the adventure and the pain of incarnation.

However, there is another leap into separateness after birth as an individual soul, and that is when you differentiate into male or female.

When you identify with either gender, you move even further away from the oneness, because in principle, the soul is not polarized, it is both male and female. As a soul, you have lived many lives, gained experience in various places in the universe and resided in many dimensions of density.

The material density of Earth is unlike any other place or dimension where you have been incarnated. There are more ethereal dimensions where it is easier to stay connected with your soul, where there is no separation yet between male and female. There, you are an androgynous being and experience this as very natural. If you like, you can recall the memory of what it was like to have a body that was not gendered, not polarized into either male or female form. Although this androgynous state of being is more natural than the polarized one, your soul desired to experience that polarity and your creative fire pushed separation even deeper.

Like the first step, the second step—the split between male and female—was accomplished through a creative desire for fulfillment and it was accompanied with an even deeper pain and loneliness in your soul.

What you wanted to learn through this dual experience of separation is the ability to experience oneness and connection in a conscious way. In the primordial sea, you could not consciously experience unity because you were part of the sea as an undifferentiated consciousness. Your state of being was diffuse, dormant, and half-asleep. It lacked consciousness. The desire for air, for breathing, is actually the desire for consciousness. The leap to self-awareness and thus to separateness is prompted by the desire for more consciousness. Not only are you created at that moment of separation as an individual soul, but you immediately become a creator yourself, a creative soul. You are now an "I" that gains experience and in time develops the ability to make choices and transform experiences into knowledge and wisdom.

Out of this desire to expand consciousness, you connect with other conscious beings or souls, allowing for communication and interaction to occur. But there is no automatic sense of unity there, for these are all different subjective experiences, and each soul follows their own path. Unity must be brought about in a conscious way through the qualities of empathy, understanding, compassion and forgiveness.

Through birth and separation, unity initially becomes shattered and in the course of a long and profound process of evolution will be restored again through the heart. What matters to me is that the two leaps of separation that you went through as a soul were not errors or mistakes, but a creative decision that comes from the masculine aspect of the soul. I want to make this clear with reference to the second leap of separation, which led to the division into male and female, and the separation of the sexes.

The moment the soul chooses an earthly life, it chooses a sexual life, and it is born into either a female or male body. The jump into an earthly body is very intense for the soul and is experienced as an enormous narrowing of consciousness. In the celestial realms where the soul usually resides before an incarnation, there is a sense of freedom and fluidity, which is difficult to maintain in the terrestrial sphere.

When you are just starting to incarnate on Earth, you have to get used to being in a body. For that reason, the soul will often want to practice being the same sex for a while. When the soul is first born as a male, it will want to repeat it to gain experience and understand how life works in a male body on Earth.

Eventually, this soul will also want to experience female lives, to understand that perspective as well. Many, but not all souls tend to return repeatedly as cither a woman or a man. They do this partly out of habit, partly out of a desire for specialization. Specialization is also a form of separation that allows you to experience one aspect of creation in all its nuances and depths.

The one-sidedness of repeatedly incarnating as either male or female gives you the opportunity to experience separation, and the pain of incompleteness. That seems paradoxical; why would you seek out that pain? The deeper the soul experiences separation and gets lost in duality and disconnection, the greater the desire for unity, for a return to connection with the Whole. When the pain of this desire becomes enveloped in consciousness, it is transformed into a creative energy which creates love.

Love is recognizing yourself in the other. Even if the other person comes to you in a completely different form, with a different gender or body, or with a completely distinct perspective, when you love, you connect with the other on a level that transcends the differences. You connect with the core of the other, the soul's spark of consciousness that is unique and yet the same. You feel warmth, involvement, and compassion in your heart, and transcend the differences by communicating, understanding, and forgiving.

This evolution towards love is the ultimate goal of the leap(s) into separation. With regard to the love between man and woman, the separation of the sexes invites the exploration of romance, infatuation, and sexuality. The desire for unification between the sexes is a creative desire, and it becomes deeply joyful when it is a dance between souls who carry opposite polarities, but at the same time recognize the Oneness in each other. Then the struggle ends, and you can enjoy the combination of unity and diversity, connecting and standing on your own.

The split between male and female on the physical level creates the possibility of love between the sexes. It forces the soul, from the deep desire for unification, to communicate consciously and vulnerably with the other, understand each other and get to know each other intimately.

In this way, separation can lead to a deeper level of awareness and love than would have been possible had you incarnated on Earth as an androgynous being. This enrichment is not only there for yourself and the other person, but it is also a source of inspiration in a broader sense that nourishes art, literature, and music.

The creative fire of the soul leads to the adventure of incarnating into a female or male body, and this separation can be exciting and joyful, but also lead to pain, isolation, and suffering. The second step of separation, the split between male and female has undeniably brought great pain in your history. When there is too much identification with the masculine or feminine, the connection with your soul is lost leaving space for division and alienation to arise between men and women. This has happened throughout human history. Many of you are wounded by this and still bring those wounds into your relationships, including your sexual ones. At times, you became deeply disappointed in life on Earth and have experienced the sharp pain of separation. Sometimes this leads to your desire to withdraw from the earthly plane. You yearn for the warm safety, and the effortless oneness of the primordial sea of which I spoke earlier.

I want to say something to those who yearn for this and experience resistance to earthly life. Remember that in addition to your desire for oneness, there has always been a desire to become self-aware and conscious. Think of your emergence from the water for that first breath. You wanted to live, you wanted to become aware, you wanted to become an individual and evolve. When the pain of being on earth takes hold of you and becomes too much, you are denying that creative fire within yourself. You want to go back to the primordial soup and dissolve into it. But your real journey is not to go backwards, your true destination is before you and the purpose is twofold: to experience connectedness and unity, and at the same time, awareness, and self-realization—being your unique self and becoming aware of your own divinity.

To put you in touch with both connectedness and separation, with both the feminine and masculine aspects of your soul, I ask you to go into your heart. Take a conscious breath into the space of your heart where love is born, and your pain is surrounded with gentleness and understanding. Ask yourself, "What have I historically chosen to be as a soul? A strong identification with the masculine or a strong identification with the feminine?" What has your soul become most accustomed to being? For a moment, note how that feels. Also feel how a certain imbalance may have arisen if you have developed too much feminine or too much masculine energy.

Now imagine meeting your inner beloved. This is the part of your soul that remained in the background when you identified with a particular gender. For example, when you become a woman in an incarnation, the male part of your soul stays behind in the sense that it becomes less manifest. Your feminine energy will be physically and emotionally more dominant, your masculine energy remains, as it were, in heaven, in the realm of the soul.

Connect now with the part of your soul that has remained more in the background during your incarnations. See this part, which appears to you as a man or a woman as a bridge to your wholeness as a soul. Look at him or her. Feel that the presence of your inner beloved is an anchor that stabilizes you. Feel it flowing through your body, your energy field, and let it ground and center you. If you lean more strongly towards feminine energy, the masculine energy of your inner beloved will balance you. Conversely, if you naturally lean more towards the masculine energy, feel more comfortable with it, then your soul's feminine energy will ground and calm you.

In the current stage of your development as a soul, most of you are restoring the unity between the opposites within yourself. You will increasingly experience the feminine and the masculine as poles that are both present in you. That is because you have grown in consciousness, put the separation into perspective and have deeply connected to your soul. You are integrating your earthly experiences. At the end of your journey through separation, having gone through the first and second leap of faith, you come to self-realization: you become a conscious "I" and at the same time you are connected to everything and everyone around you through your heart. You accept the masculine and the feminine in yourself, your being one—unique, autonomous, and your Being One—connected, transcending yourself, part of the Whole.

Chapter 2- Integrate your masculine energy

Jeshua distinguishes between ego-based and heart-based awareness in both the male and the female energy which have a light and a shadow side. He emphasizes how important it is to recognize and integrate the mature, heart-based version of masculine energy, especially when you have a sensitive feminine energy which lacks boundaries.

I am Jeshua, your brother and friend.

I would like to talk to you about masculine energy and integrating it into your everyday consciousness. This is important for both women and men.

This world is in the midst of a transition from ego to heart, from consciousness based on fear and lack, to consciousness based on compassion and abundance. Letting go of fear-based consciousness is particularly challenging on the human level as it has become a habit and a way of surviving for many centuries. However, fear-based consciousness is deeply destructive, it is always looking for power and control, and hence leads to struggle and competition between people. Nature is subjugated by this form of consciousness and is exhausted by it.

The energies of fear, control, and power block the free expression of the soul in earthly reality. The soul thrives on openness, joy, and freedom. Without these heart energies, a human being withers like a flower without water and light. People are suffering collectively because they are disconnected from their souls. There is widespread mental, psychological, and emotional suffering caused by the sickening effects of fear, worry and lack of love. If you don't feel in touch with your soul, you can't be truly inspired and experience life as meaningful.

The need for change is intensifying worldwide. It presents itself in many ways—natural disasters, disease, poverty, and war all show how collective consciousness functions and how it is largely in the grip of fear and control. Crises can, however, invite deep reflection and awareness of the causes of suffering.

In your world, it is becoming increasingly clear that the old model of leadership, based on authority, coercion, and control is failing and backfiring. Authoritarian forms of leadership are still omnipresent, but on the inner, psychological level, a reversal is beginning to take place in the collective consciousness. There is growing resistance to traditional forms of male leadership, and the masculine energy itself is now being questioned in a thorough and fundamental way.

The ego or fear-based masculine energy is out of touch with the heart and with the feminine qualities of empathy, connection, and compassion. This leads to a disrespectful, almost mechanical way of dealing with life—people, animals and plants are treated as merely a means to an end. Today's achievement-and-success oriented global culture of production and consumption is literally inhuman. It ignores the human dimension and the fragility of life. More people realize this, but there is still the lack of a clear alternative and vision for the new.

It is necessary to redefine the masculine energy in such a way that masculinity is understood to be naturally connected with, instead of opposed to, the feminine. There needs to be room for a masculine energy that does not seek to subjugate or control people and nature, but rather serve the common good out of a sense of truth, wisdom, and clarity. Such a higher, mature masculine energy exists, although it is not easily recognized. It has long been a "forbidden energy" without a place for expression in cultures dominated by ego-based male power structures.

I myself was a forbidden male. I didn't fit into the authoritarian society I lived in and clashed with the male ego energy there. My fate was not unique. There were always outsiders who criticized the collective consciousness and argued for more equality, love, and compassion. The mature, power-free masculine energy is an energy of the heart, and this heart-based masculine energy is present in both men and women. It is important that the existence and character of this masculine energy is more widely recognized and understood. New definitions are needed, as are examples and role models of heart-based masculine energy.

A clear distinction should be made between ego-based and heart-based masculine energy. The same should be done with regard to femininity because it also has a dark and a light variant. Both poles are fueled by fear and ego, or by love and trust. Heart-based masculine energy is loving, is respectful of the vulnerable and honors the feminine. At the same time, it is not feminine energy. The higher masculine energy is characterized by truthfulness, focus and clarity. These are masculine qualities which can be embodied equally by women. Masculine energy creates distinctions and boundaries based on truthfulness. It is by nature one-pointed and focused, leading to clarity and insight at the heart level. The feminine energy is by its nature connecting and transcending, which leads to love and compassion at the heart level, qualities that can also be embodied by men.

Because you know the ego-based variety of masculine energy, which leans on fear, power and control, the higher variety is not familiar to you. In the absence of mature masculinity, feminine energy is sometimes idealized, and considered to be morally superior. It is gentle and loving, an antidote to aggressive masculinity, and this creates a contradiction between the masculine and feminine.

A stereotypical image has emerged of an abusive, masculine ego energy on the one hand, and a caring feminine heart energy on the other. It seems that these are the only alternatives. This image is incorrect, however, and oversimplified. It is also harmful because 1) by insufficiently recognizing the male heart energy, you cannot integrate and use it properly, and 2) by insufficiently recognizing the female ego energy, you cannot release and use it properly.

I'll start with the second point. There are two varieties of feminine energy: the heart-based, higher variety which is empathetic, gentle, and wise, and the ego-based variety, which operates from emptiness, lack of independence, and lack of self-esteem. The feminine energy in the fear-based form can become manipulative, suffocating, blaming and resentful. I will not discuss the dark side of the feminine energy any further, now. I will focus mainly on defining heart-based masculine energy. What I would like to emphasize with regard to the second point is that in order to have a clear understanding of masculine versus feminine energy, one must distinguish between the ego and the heart-based version in both.

The transition from ego to heart is not a transition from male to female; both energies need to be lifted to the heart-based, higher variant. To grow from ego-based to heart-based consciousness also means transforming and releasing the fear-based feminine energy within yourself. (This theme is discussed at length in the book The Forbidden Female Speaks).

To the first point, how do you recognize and integrate the masculine heart energy? Above, I mentioned some of the qualities associated with this energy, and now I will speak more visually about it, so that your imagination and your feelings are engaged.

Imagine that there is a knight in your heart. See if you can visualize a self-aware and centered masculine personality in the center of your heart, wielding a sword, radiating both strength and love. You sense a particular form of leadership and self-confidence in him, and at the same time compassion and understanding. His vision, his focus, his decisiveness does not exclude but includes everything, considers different perspectives and considerations. He is not dominant or controlling, but clear. He oversees the whole, he does not obscure. There is something piercing, honest, and sobering about his presence.

Take this figure in and look at it. How does this heart-based masculine energy affect you? Do you feel how it belongs to you? This energetic presence that you feel and perceive is not something or someone outside of you. This energy is yours. It belongs to your soul, whether you are male or female. Masculine and feminine energies are qualities of the soul. Both men and women have become estranged from the heart-based masculine energy. You have seen too few examples of it in your lives. Your fathers were often either authoritarian and domineering or absent and emotionally closed.

Many of you are sensitive and empathetic to others. This often means that you can lose touch with yourself when you're with them. Your boundaries easily get blurry, and you have difficulty staying true to your own needs in relationships—with a partner, family, or colleagues. When your masculine energy is not functioning properly, you often feel unable to assume your own space, resulting in exhaustion, anger, or disappointment. This is a situation that often arises with extremely sensitive, empathetic women and men.

Imagine that you say YES to your masculine heart energy. It flows through you, and you feel its loving, warm, protective power. You may experience it as fatherly, an encouraging and wise masculine energy. Sense if there are particular parts of your energy field, of your body, that need this energy. What happens to you when you allow this masculine energy to flow through you? You may feel that as a result, you distance yourself from situations or people that drain or upset you. If you are inclined to easily absorb the energy of other people, especially the people you love and care about, it can throw you off balance, and too often erase your sense of self. The masculine energy reminds you to focus on YOU. What do I feel right now? What do I need? The masculine energy helps you reclaim your own space.

Imagine that there is an energetic space around you that is yours. It belongs to you alone. Now, command energies that are not yours—pain, emotion, the worries of other people—to leave this space. Do it with ease and confidence. Remember that to push these "alien" energies out doesn't mean you don't care about your loved ones. It means that you are at home inside your own space and from this home base enter into a relationship with the outside world, and other people.

Connect with your root chakra, the energy center at the bottom of your spine near your tailbone. Become aware of your legs as they connect you to the earth. Then put your focus on your crown chakra at the very top of your head. Feel the energy of your own soul. You are here on earth with a specific set of intentions and goals. Feel how the soul focuses on this particular path you walk, and how your soul's energy wants to flow down through you in a vertical axis from crown to tailbone. Your masculine energy, the knight in your heart, helps you keep this channel open and clean. The knight protects that space you need in order to connect with yourself and focus on your goals.

Bow to yourself. Be aware of your own space.

Take care of yourself and respect your own masculine sense of boundaries.

Chapter 3- The energetic origins of fatigue

Jeshua speaks about fatigue and its causes. Psychological overload and self-denial are the real causes, not physical exertion. He discusses the energetic reasons behind this kind of fatigue, common among sensitive and spiritually aware people. To prevent and treat fatigue, it is important to use your masculine heart energy—to be true to your deepest impulses, to set limits, and dare to be different.

I am Jeshua, your brother and friend.

I would like to speak to you about fatigue. As you develop spiritually, you become more aware of the energies around you, more sensitive and perceptive of the emotional energies in yourself and in others. Many of you lose energy when you are "in the world." You feel tired and drained when you are in certain places or in the presence of certain people. This fatigue has energetic origins of a non-physical nature. It costs you energy-wise to be in the world when you have a level of awareness that does not match up with the energetic vibration of the world.

When you enter this reality, your consciousness is different from mainstream collective consciousness. Fear and power-based survival mechanisms have dominated mainstream consciousness for a long time. It is part of your soul's path to bring in something new because you do not fit with mainstream society. Your energetic frequency is more attuned to the heart and focused on transitioning from ego to heart. This focus on renewal and transformation means that you can partially adapt, but not fully, to what is considered to be normal. You often notice from an early age that it is difficult to take on the habits, morals and expectations of your parents and family. You also notice this difficulty at school and in the workplace.

As you enter adulthood, many of you realize that you are walking a different path than other people, that you tend to ask deeper questions about life and don't accept easy answers. You want to know why life is the way it is. You are interested in the meaning of it all, and why you are here. It is part of your nature to persistently question and investigate this.

Heart-based consciousness has awakened in you. Even as a child you felt "something is off" in the so-called normal world of adults. Rules and values dictated how one should behave, feel, and think, and these rules and moral stances, implicitly full of judgments, are instilled in you from an early age. You absorb them non-verbally and energetically. There is something inside of you that resists this and a deep part of you wonders why people impose these rules on themselves? Why do they wear masks and hide their true feelings?

You sense a hidden emotional layer in people that they dare not speak of because they were taught to be ashamed of it. Yet, you are acutely aware of what they suppress, and thus, receive conflicting information. On the one hand, the official truth, which corresponds with rules and social expectations, and on the other hand, the hidden truth which corresponds to emotions that are underground but that you are able to tune into vibrationally. You feel that this vibration is truer than the official masks people wear and present to you.

Initially, you possessed a clear radar for these underground emotions, but this ability sometimes got you in trouble and you chose to suppress it, however, you were able to sense the truth. When you did use it, follow it, and act on it, your behavior changed and there were consequences to this. You wanted to fit in, be liked, succeed in life so you suppressed this power of perception.

When you suppress your sensitivity and your ability to sense the truth, you lower your vibration to a frequency that does not correspond with your natural frequency. You go against your soul and suppress the most evolved part of yourself, and this can make you feel extremely tired. This fatigue does not come from physical exertion, it comes from self-denial.

You have a pure, truth-oriented sensitivity within you that yearns to be recognized. There is something in your core that does not fit this reality, and I am asking you to allow this original pure sensitivity to return. You are afraid to do this because you expect to be judged for it. However, the price you pay for not allowing in what you know and feel to be true is high; you cut yourself off from your own light.

The moment your soul's light is thwarted, it cannot flow through your heart and body. This is when you lose vitality, and when you withdraw your soul's energy, it causes an energetic fatigue. You are no longer yourself. Instead, you are full of fear, and the vibration of fear is exhausting. You lose yourself in the world around you and become fatigued due to your empathic abilities as well.

As a soul who is awake at the heart level, you have a natural ability to attune to the feelings and moods of those around you. You can sense how someone is feeling and that's okay. It is when you act on the impulse to help and alleviate the suffering of the other person that you take a wrong turn. It is humane and sweet to want to help, but if you try too hard to solve someone else's problems, you will feel exhausted, and this indicates that something is not right.

Ask yourself this question: Can the person whose suffering you feel, receive your help and are you attuned to what he or she needs? You can be overzealous in offering help when it may be wiser not to reach out or interfere. What the other person needs from you is your energetic presence, your pure frequency, and a sense of truth unclouded by the fearful energies of this world.

You do the other person, and the world at large, a service if you stay true to your core, and not get hooked into a heavy sense of responsibility, and excessive caring. Allow the person to stumble and make mistakes. You don't have to feel obligated to carry their pain and suffering. The function of your sensitivity is not to absorb and carry the pain and suffering of others, but rather to hold the vibration of truth. You do that not by descending into their suffering but by putting limits on how much you help.

When someone shows you their dark side in an honest way and reveals the hidden pain under their official mask, this is the first step towards their self-knowledge and liberation. Your role is to be present with the other person and to welcome their shadow side with compassion. That is vastly different than stepping in and thinking you can alleviate or dissolve their pain for them.

Use your feminine ability to connect and empathize coupled with your masculine ability to remain in your own energy space. You do not absorb their energy of pain and suffering, but you do surround it with clear awareness. Your feminine energy allows you to tune into the other, the world around you; your masculine energy helps you stay aware of yourself, your own vibration, and your own needs.

If you manage to hold on to your masculine energy while interacting with the world, you will immediately note when you start to get tired. You are alert to yourself, and to interactions between you and other people. It is then that you can intervene, but you can also withdraw when you start to feel tired and move away from a situation or an environment that drains and depletes you. At times, you let yourself linger in these situations out of fear. However, the light of your soul does not thrive on fear, duty, and guilt. It thrives on joy and inspiration. If you are extremely sensitive and at the same time act from guilt, shame, duty, and obligation, then the situation you are in will exhaust you to the maximum. It is not your sensitivity itself that is the culprit. It is the pressure you put upon yourself to stay and help in certain situations. The judgment that comes with this is the real source of your fatigue.

Your degree of sensitivity is an achievement for your soul. You cannot and do not have to change it. What you do want to change is the extent to which you are still controlled by fear—fear of letting your light shine, and fear of saying "no" to the heavy burden of carrying the sorrow of others. You need to correct your perception of what role you play in helping others, and what it truly means to share your light.

Many old religious doctrines taught people to believe that they are small and sinful and need rules outside themselves to find their way. This longstanding tradition totally negates the original creative power of your soul, which attracts what is fruitful for you. This creative power belongs to you. It is free and sparkling like a river of bubbling, vitalizing water. This power is not concerned with control or coercion. This power stream has a great driving force, and at the same time is playful and intuitive in a subtle way.

Your soul expresses itself through feelings of inspiration and joy. That is why it is important to notice when you sense signs of tiredness and exhaustion, especially if they persist and go hand in hand with a lack of pleasure and zest for life. These are signs from your soul that indicate you are denying yourself something and you need to address it.

In summary, there are two causes of energetic fatigue: when you adapt yourself to others out of fear of rejection, and when you give too much and absorb someone else's suffering. In both cases, you must focus on your own pure core, your original light, and use your masculine energy to hold space. If you connect too much with the world out of fear, you step into the trap of ego-based feminine energy: you act from an inner emptiness and lack of self-awareness. You identify with the role of helper or caretaker, you respond to outside expectations, and you diminish your light. It is then that you are living according to an idea of how it should be: you are sweet, accommodating, and helpful. Breaking free from this framework seems wrong and selfish, but if you don't, you are no longer free to play, and create from your heart.

What you need in order to liberate yourself from this moral straitjacket is your higher masculine energy, especially the qualities of courage, insight, and defiance. Then, you can detach from the self-denying pressure you put on yourself. The more you do this, the more vitality you will feel.

Another reason you experience energetic fatigue stems from a lack of peace and simplicity, and not spending enough time in nature. Your soul needs to regularly withdraw from the world to process and recover from the turmoil and intense emotional energies that surround you. To be in an atmosphere of peace and quiet is highly conducive to hearing and feeling the original whispers of your soul. There are many heavy, negative, and dramatic energies in the world, and they weigh on you, even though you may not notice them because you have grown used to it.

Nature radiates a vibration of peace and balance and brings you into contact with a more natural rhythm of life that fits better with the flow of your soul. Sensitive people have a deep need for silence and rest. If you don't meet that need, you will feel exhausted and fail to take care of yourself.

Silence is the cradle of creativity. I don't mean physical silence; I mean finding the inner space where you can withdraw and reflect on your emotions and thoughts. This is easier to do in an environment that is conducive to being still. Silence invites you to slow down, relax and access your inner depths. To find stillness is an inhalation for the soul. The soul connects to its original knowledge and insight, and inspiration arises from this connection.

Some people feel threatened by silence, afraid to create it for themselves, because there are no distractions to keep painful emotions from bubbling up. Fatigue is a way to not feel anything. News, social media, and a busy schedule are ways to overload yourself with impressions which are numbing and can eventually lead to exhaustion.

If you really take time and space for yourself, you will notice that you have to change the course of your life, and this can evoke fear—fear of rejection, fear of change, fear of hurting people. But the only way to live a life full of vitality and inspiration is by facing your fear. Peace, quiet and simplicity are your friends. They help you become aware of your original nature; they are oxygen for the soul.

Energetic fatigue is the language the soul uses to call your attention to something. Let it be an invitation to consult your masculine heart energy and be in touch with what you truly need, what brings you joy, what you might let go of. Dare to live freely from your heart and soul.

Chapter 4- See clearly from your heart

In the previous chapter, Jeshua emphasized the importance of creating space for yourself and connecting with your soul's light and wisdom. By allowing your masculine energy to shield you from an excess of outside impressions, you automatically start living more from intuition and your own wisdom. You develop the ability to see clearly.

In this chapter, Jeshua discusses what clairvoyance is—not a supernatural gift, but a natural expression of evolving heart consciousness. The more you let go of judgments and fears, the more you become attuned to your soul.

I am Jeshua, your brother and soul mate.

Sensitivity, which I discussed in the previous chapter, is related to clairvoyance. Both develop spontaneously when awakening to heart-based consciousness but can only flourish if you're able to shield yourself from the chaotic, confused energies in the world and in your mind. Your masculine energy is the sword that shields you and allows you to tune into your soul. I will talk about this attunement; what keeps you from it and how to rekindle it.

To develop clairvoyance is not something supernatural or a special gift that you may or may not have. It is an ability that develops naturally as you become more attuned to your inner self, to looking within and being aware of what is there.

You were born into a human body with five senses. You perceive the world physically through your eyes, your ears, your sense of touch and your ability to smell and taste. They bring you in close contact with the physical, earthly reality. This is a precious ability because physical life gives you the opportunity to experience life intensely. You experience pleasure and pain, and as a soul incarnated in a body, you also experience an array of different moods, feelings and emotional ups and downs, all of which the soul finds valuable.

Your human mind is full of thoughts. During your childhood, your parents, family, school, workplace, and the world around you handed down and filled your mind with ideas and beliefs. These thoughts, which contain a mixture of judgments and perceptions, have an enormous influence on how you experience life. They function as a filter that molds your feelings and emotions. When you absorb your parents' worldview, emotional traces remain with you. This can be a burden for you because most worldviews are fraught with fears of survival, pain, lack, and death. The fear of rejection is strong. Parents effortlessly and unconsciously pass this on to their children even though they don't mean to.

What I described here about being human, is the outer layer of who you are. Your senses originate in the body, and ideas and beliefs stem from outside yourself. How you react to the forming of your emotional world is something that partly escapes that outer layer. Every child is different with a unique way of responding to the world. The child's inner world is not causally determined by what he or she has absorbed from the outside world.

When you enter earthly life, your soul is receptive to everything you experience during the first years of childhood. But from the beginning, there is an inner flame there, a presence that is independent of this outer layer, separate from the outer environment. Pure clairvoyance is the ability to make and maintain contact with that inner flame. This aspect of yourself, this core, has always been there way before this lifetime. You respond in an original way to the world around you, to what presents itself in your current life, because of your soul's core. How you react from that original core, that flame of your soul's consciousness, says something about your life path, about what your soul intends to do and experience here.

It is extremely important to stay connected with this inner part of yourself because it gives meaning to everything you do and experience. It also gives direction to your life when things don't turn out how you wanted or expected them to, or how the outside world expected them to.

Your soul's knowledge is contained in that inner flame and has its own logic. Being in tune with this logic is essential to your happiness, a happiness that is there in a joyful, deep way. It is not something superficial. Happiness in this sense means to be in harmony with who you are and what you came to do in this life. This differs a great deal from the kinds of images and expectations that the outside world presents to you as happiness.

Clairvoyance is an attunement to the soul, to the inner logic of the soul. When you are attuned, the soul will show you how to follow your life path. It is also possible for you to attune to the soul of another. If you sense and see from the heart, you can perceive things that relate to yourself and to others.

What exactly is pure clairvoyance, this ability to intuitively see from the heart? It happens when you connect with your inner flame, your core, and observe a situation with an open mind and a quiet heart. This does not involve using preconceived notions about how something should be, for example, judgments, expectations or wishes. It means to observe without any thought or emotion. Pure clairvoyance or intuition wells up from a silent space. It cannot flourish where excessive thinking, rigid views, or strong emotions are present.

Consider this—if you have a fervent desire for something, you may fall into wishful thinking to attain it. You tell yourself that certain things are bound to happen, and that you can intuitively see the future. In truth, you see a future that you want to have and this powerful wish influences you and your perception of things. You best be on your guard!

When you perceive a powerful emotion or expectation within yourself, it is best to focus inwardly on the emotion itself and ask if there is any fear underlying it. It is more useful to focus on this than on what may or may not happen. It is more important for your inner growth to find out why you are in the grip of a particular emotion than to know the future (which you cannot).

Clairvoyance that flows from the heart is not a tool to predict the future. That's not its purpose. For one, the future is not fixed. Life is not about knowing what events will or will not take place. There is a range of possibilities and paths available for you to take. Life is about developing yourself on the inner level. You automatically attract situations or encounters that match the life path your soul wants to walk. The soul wants to go through certain experiences and gain a deep understanding of them. The soul doesn't want to avoid negative experiences per se and only experience positive ones. No! The soul wants to consciously experience both, thereby deepening its understanding and wisdom. The soul grows and evolves from this kind of learning experience and when it does, you start to naturally attract more positive experiences into your life. Joy is natural to the soul.

Clairvoyance is a natural ability which is within all human beings, but it calls for being attuned to your Self, to your inner core, to your heart. What stands in the way of connecting to it are your thoughts and emotions. Thoughts and emotions are not bad or wrong, but they are often unaligned with your inner core. They can be restless and unstable. In order to clearly perceive things, you have to know how to quiet yourself and become still.

I invite you to descend into your core where your inner flame dwells. Let go of your thoughts, the peaks, the valleys of your emotions. Let them go to the periphery of who you are—after all, that's where they belong. Thoughts and emotions are part of your human consciousness. Allow them to be there. But right now, you are going inside your core of inner knowing. Take your attention away from your thoughts. Let them go. Become aware of your breathing and breathe deeply into your abdomen. Imagine that with every breath, your emotions and concerns are given air and space. Let go of your fears for a while and be free. Remember, you are free.

The moment you go inside with your attention, and become aware of your breathing, you can sense a space opening in your heart. Imagine a temple there or a beautiful place in nature. It's quiet there. You may feel the soft rustling of the wind or hear the babbling of a brook, tender sounds that take you deeper inside yourself. Distance yourself from the noise of your thoughts and the turbulent waters of your emotions. Experience the power of silence. This place you retreat to in your heart is quiet in a sweet and welcoming way.

Rest in that beautiful place. Remember how rich your soul is, how much you already know and have experienced. You don't need to constantly feed on outside ideas, opinions, and beliefs that you hear or read in newspapers or the media. Be still. Connect with your intuitive knowing. It comes from within. Your heart and soul have evolved throughout many lifetimes. You have gone through deep experiences. The inner flame in your heart connects you to a much greater whole, which transcends the earthly.

You have guides, you have a soul family. They connect you to sources of wisdom that transcend your human mind and continually provide you with help and assistance. Feel the light and gentleness of these sources. There are beings of light – you may call them guides, teachers or friends—who are there for you on the inner plane. You are never alone. Even though you may feel physically alone, there is spiritual help at your side in the deepest darkness.

You think that only people with a special gift can see or communicate with these beings of light, who offer you help and guidance. That is not true. Each of you can do this in your own way. Turning inward and reconnecting with stillness opens you to other dimensions of being, to your own inner knowing. It is a natural ability that everyone has. The more you want it and are prepared to go into the depths of your own being, the easier it becomes. You don't need any special gift. You are primarily a soul. The reality of the soul is yours. It is your reality.

Again, become aware of the silent space in your heart, and be in that beautiful temple or quiet place in nature, and look! Someone is coming toward you! It is a radiant being, a guide or an angel who warmly smiles at you. The being who radiates kindness and joy comes closer and nods to you. You recognize him or her. Something in their appearance touches your heart and lights up your spirit. Simply experience the loving presence of this guide. Feel how their radiance flows into your heart. Feel how you perceive this intuitively, not with your earthly senses, nor with your thoughts, but from an open heart that perceives with purity and no expectations.

Now the guide or angel sits down next to you and puts his or her hand on your heart, either on your back or on your chest. Observe what happens. What do you feel when that hand touches your heart? Allow it, perceive it—joy, grief, relief, whatever it is. The guide who is with you would like to make you aware of something. What is it? What is this guide reminding you of? Feel it, sense it. Be calm and quiet and take in the message that your guide has for you. It can come in the shape of a word, an image, or a feeling. Let it flow into you, heart to heart, and absorb the energy of this message which contains truth and wisdom.

When you look into the eyes of this guide and say goodbye, you become aware once again of the deep silence inside your heart. Feel your body and the earth beneath you. Consciously allow the energy of Mother Earth to flow into your feet and legs. You feel grounded and are back in the here and now.

When you grasp things with your intuition, an inner shift takes place from outside to inside, from the usual emotional turmoil to the calm center. That is the key to seeing clearly from the heart. There is a difference between using your intuition (seeing clearly from the heart) and being psychically aware of the energies surrounding you. What do I mean by this?

In your everyday life, energies of the human collective made up of common beliefs, prejudices, fears, and emotions constantly surround you. This collective atmosphere is like an energy field that surrounds the earth: a collective field of human thoughts, beliefs, and emotions. This field surrounds and affects you like the weather can. It affects your moods and thoughts. It is not neutral, on the contrary, it is full of fear and judgment.

When people make psychic predictions or think they receive clairvoyant impressions, it may well be that they are psychic, but when they are simply "picking up" images, fearful thoughts, or strong emotions from this collective field, what they perceive is not based on truth or clarity. What they tune into are fear-based and "hungry" astral energies, which may belong to deceased people who linger in this atmosphere close to earth after they die.

The astral (non-physical, energetic) dimension around the earth is not just created and fueled by peoples' thoughts and feelings who are on earth. Souls that have crossed over to the other side are actively present in this astral field. They still cling to earthly reality, and wander in that dimension because they have not found a way to free themselves. They are earthbound souls. A person can make contact clairvoyantly with the astral field, but the information can be misleading, based on fear or judgment even though it may appear loving and wise on the surface. A subtle power or manipulative energy is present there.

The density and heaviness in the astral field that surrounds the earth is quite different from the wisdom of your soul. You may not notice that these astral energies can manipulate you, but you can and do get caught up in these thought forms. They can be seductive, and it is easy to get carried away by the sweeping stories of good and evil and "the battle between light and dark." The astral plane feeds on duality and emotional drama.

How do you distinguish between information that is heart-based and clear, and information that is fear or power-based? Your heart is the key. The heart is the seat of wisdom. To be in that heart space, you need to become still, free from emotional turmoil and limiting beliefs. That's why you need to know yourself, know your own shadow (pain, fear), before you can open up to the truth.

As you get familiar with heart-based consciousness, you start to sense which intuitive messages come from joy and truthfulness, and which ones aren't truly intuitive and come from illusion, fear, and desire. Always tune into the emotional charge or undercurrent of any psychic message. Never put authority outside yourself. Trust yourself and know that there is a sacred space within your heart, an inner flame, which can lift you above the astral plane, away from the collective consciousness. It connects you to universal wisdom, to truth, to the home of your soul and from there, you see clearly.

Part II- The forbidden male speaks

Chapter 5- Masculinity and femininity: caged dancers

The next five chapters will be a dialogue between Jeshua and me, a conversation which started after the publication of my book *The Forbidden Female Speaks*, when I received so many responses from men who had recognized their own wounds while reading the book. I realized that the story of the injured, disempowered woman had to be supplemented with an explanation of how men were also wounded.

In the following dialogue, consisting of a Q & A with Jeshua, he addresses the differences between masculine and feminine energy, the wounding of the male, how to recognize and heal it, and the importance of heart-based masculine energy for both men *and* women.

My questions to Jeshua are in italics.

Jeshua, what would you like to tell us about male energy, the forbidden male, the wounded man?

In creation at large, there is a natural energy that you call masculine, just as there is a natural energy that you call feminine. You are aware that male energy exists in your reality, but masculinity truly exists independently of how people think about it and the boxes they put it in and the definitions that are placed on it. As a soul, every human being is a mixture of masculine and feminine, two in one. A person's physical sexuality only partially determines their unique character and personality.

The traditional definition of masculinity is one-sided and limiting. It implies that men must restrict their emotional self-expression, which in turn makes it difficult for them to connect with their soul. This one-dimensional view of masculinity that has dominated much of your history is rooted in a consciousness based on fear and the need for power. This form of masculine energy was used to control and conquer life. Feminine energy was seen as the chaotic, unpredictable, and emotional side of being human that had to be controlled. Internally, men were forced to control their emotions and externally, women were relegated to a second-class position in society.

You're saying that, first, the soul is not masculine or feminine but is made up of both energies, and second, that the traditional definition of masculinity which men have had to live with has emotionally wounded them and created a distorted dichotomy between men and women.

Indeed, but first I will speak about the soul and how it encompasses both poles, the masculine and the feminine and at the same time transcends them. Then, I will address the emotional wounding in men.

At its deepest core, the soul is pure consciousness that is unique and individual. The soul has the powerful ability to create because it is imbued with something completely new. As an example, when you make bread, it is a fresh loaf every time made according to a standard recipe and a fixed list of ingredients. It is a copy of previous loaves, but unlike the making of bread, when the soul is created, it has a unique spark within it that is irreducibly original. This spark does not come from a compiled, fixed list of "basic parts." The soul is individual. It is self-contained, and autonomous with its own original tone and color. It stands on its own.

This is a miracle.

The soul is creative and is free to create on its own. This individual divine spark within you has a consciousness that makes choices based on its own experiences. The very existence of the soul is a great miracle. It is the ultimate creative act of God—the creation of a being that is free, autonomous, unique, and can create just like God creates. Our soul came into being out of this love and trust. As the earth gives birth to life, and the mother gives birth to a child, so the soul is cast into the world confident that the seed within it will bud, blossom, and bring forth a new consciousness that will enrich all of creation.

Because of the unique spark in each soul, generic descriptions can never capture the essence of someone's soul. Psychological theories can explain human behavior, some of which define distinctive character types and temperaments, but the deep individuality of a person remains a divine mystery.

If you accept that this mystery exists and acknowledge how deep the mystery is, you realize that to define yourself as male or female is limiting. There are universal, archetypal energies such as male/female, young/old, active/passive, introvert/extrovert. But who you really are cannot be defined by combining a limited list of biological and psychological characteristics even if you use complex belief systems such as astrology, the Enneagram, or personality theory. They can provide valuable information that may help you understand yourself better, but mainly they explain how you are conditioned on a personality level and how certain survival mechanisms cause you to act in a particular way because they have a hold on you. Your unique core is divine and indeterminate. To realize this is of immense importance.

When you realize that you are God-like—free and creative—you perceive yourself differently. Although you have a male or female body and have been influenced by definitions of what constitutes masculinity and femininity, these biological and psychological characteristics can never capture who you are.

To connect with your unique core again, you must let go of all these limiting definitions and accept the miracle that is you. You are a creator. No law exists outside of you that can determine what you can or will do. When you understand that you are free to create, you will also understand how oppressive the social conditioning is that has been imposed on you as a man or a woman. This conditioning is born out of fear and ignorance, and it denies you your freedom and individuality.

You started by saying that a distortion of the soul occurs when definitions of masculinity are based on fear and the need for control. Can you explain what you mean by this, and what a more accurate definition of masculinity would be?

I would like to expand on the idea or definition of masculine energy and clarify the original meaning and purpose of it in Creation at large. Most men lost touch with their souls when they tried to conform to the false expectations regarding masculinity. The existing definitions of masculinity are commonplace and have been imposed for centuries on the male consciousness. Men felt trapped by them and struggled with their own self-imposed expectations of having to be perfect and comply at the cost of their well-being. There is a great need to reflect on what constitutes true masculinity.

To this end, I would like to distinguish between the two forms or levels of masculinity and femininity. From this broader, layered framework, I will clarify how to redefine masculinity or femininity, lift it to the level of the soul thereby freeing yourself from the straitjacket which imprisons you.

I call the two kinds of masculinity original and destructive. Likewise, there is original and destructive femininity. The original masculine and feminine energy emanate from the level of the soul, the heart. At this level, the masculine and feminine energies are two faces of the One; organically connected, functioning in close coherence with each other. God is masculine and feminine at the same time.

Original masculine energy can focus, disconnect, and also create fragmentation, in other words—plurality and diversity. The material world was born from the One because of this same exact power to focus and disconnect. Masculine energy is responsible for creating diversity and individuality. The One fragmented into a multitude of forms separated in time and space.

In the beginning, when consciousness was not in a state of focus, not experiencing itself as separate from the whole (the One), it was expansive, oceanic and all encompassing. This is the feminine aspect of Creation. At one end of the divine spectrum, there is the indeterminate, the non-individualized, the undifferentiated field of Oneness that connects everything. There are no dividing lines. There is unity but also immobility, a lack of movement. This is the feminine aspect of creation.

The masculine energy breaks up the Unity, and consciousness becomes individualized at some point in space, like an ocean breaking apart into separate drops. This is how the soul, your individual soul, is born. You are a mix of Oneness and Separateness, of feminine and masculine. You were born from this Unity, from the womb of the Ocean and became a droplet with a consciousness of your own, an inalienable, unique self.

In this move towards individuation—being born as an individual soul—it initially might seem that the connection with the Whole gets broken. Suddenly, you are thrust out of the womb and the separation *hurts*. The birth experience is so overwhelming for the newborn that it loses all connection with the One, the Ocean, the Mother. The connection is still there, just as the drop still belongs to the ocean, but the young soul feels the pain of separation.

That's what you talked about in chapter one and what you call cosmic birth pain in the book, The Jeshua Channelings. *Cosmic birth pain is the pain or trauma of leaving Oneness, the loss of a primal security that felt safe.*

Yes. The soul's evolutionary purpose is to come to terms with and transcend this birth pain. When this transcendence is achieved, a sense of freedom emerges within you that has integrated the masculine and feminine aspects of creation. You will be aware of Unity in everything and will simultaneously be at home with yourself as a unique and autonomous being. In the mature soul, the original male and female energies are balanced and work together creatively.

Were the masculine and feminine energies originally polar energies that together enabled the creation of individual consciousness?

Yes, with the emphasis on "together," or even better, "inextricably linked." They are polar as seen in the yin-yang symbol—they cannot exist independently of each other. The dance of male and female is creative, and the purpose of the dance is to experience the joy of creating. Just like the purpose of creating is not a means to an end, it is the end. God is not outside of creation. God is in creation and inside you. You think that God exists somewhere outside of creation, as a static being who controls or manipulates everything from a distance and who might direct or turn things around to reduce suffering or change people.

The image of God as outside of creation seems a testament to the male fantasy which is God as ruler, omnipotent, controlling, versus a passive and sinful creation. This image also conveys a kind of arbitrariness— God created the world for unclear reasons. He is perfect and created imperfection, suffering, confusion, war, violence. Why? Why does he need that creation?

The only way creation will be truly meaningful to you is when you let go of the image of God as an omnipotent, paternalistic ruler. If you do this, you will be free of the harmful notions about sin and guilt with which you are saddled. I want to especially point out the importance of understanding how the masculine and feminine energies were originally One, because it has an enormous influence on (1) how you imagine God, (2) understanding yourself as a soul that carries both of these energies inside you, and (3) how you function as a man or woman.

Would you clarify again what you mean by that original unity, and then explain these three points? It is not about literal unity, because male and female are different energies. But at the same time, they are not independent of each other. They are different, even polar, but not autonomous.

Imagine your soul as a dancer and creation as a dance. Imagine God as a dance. A dance is not static, it is a dynamic whole. Now, imagine that dance is the most essential level of existence. You can distinguish the aspects or components of the dance, but they only take on meaning within the dance itself. Separately, they are empty and dead. This applies in a comparable way to the elements of masculinity and femininity as well. Without the interplay between the two, they are nothing, they cannot function or even exist as independent elements.

Masculinity, in the sense of how it can focus and separate, only has meaning against the background of the oceanic feminine that connects everything. Applied to human beings, once the mature soul realizes that it is unique and free and yet intimately connected to the whole, thus uniting male and female within itself, the human being can finally consciously create. Then the dance of the soul that inhabits a human body becomes creative—original and joyful.

By masculine and feminine unity, you mean the organic and natural co-operation of complementary energies as are beautifully depicted in the yin-yang symbol.

Precisely. Yin and yang are about natural complementarity, about rhythm—as in the seasons, as in birth and death. Duality, on the other hand, is a false construct, a mechanistic image pasted over reality. The world is not a machine put together by a mechanic who assembles a lot of individual parts.

It is important to realize that the original masculine and feminine energies are One in this organic, complementary sense because you say this has enormous consequences for how we perceive our image of God, how we understand ourselves as a soul that carries both aspects within it, and finally how we function as a man or woman. If we understand this, we can then distinguish between original masculinity and femininity on the one hand, and destructive femininity and masculinity on the other.

It is extremely important to make this distinction, because false ideas of what constitutes the masculine and feminine profoundly influence the actions people take and can create enormous existential pain. You can hardly underestimate this influence.

Masculine and feminine energy do not exist on their own; they only function when they are organically connected in the created world, for example, in humans. What does this mean in relation to how we imagine God?

That God is not a man, God is not outside of creation, and God is not a conductor who orchestrates the dance of creation.

God is both masculine and feminine, is present inside creation and "dances with us." Could you phrase it like this?

Yes. It also means that God is inside you and that the original masculine and the original feminine are both present inside you too. Your soul is living the dance of evolution, has manifested in matter, and is discovering its own creative power as an individual spark.

I understand, so it is a mistake to think that as a man you consist of male energy and as a woman you consist of female energy.

You are indeed shaped by having either a male or a female body, but especially by environmental influences such as your parents, upbringing, society. If you were to remove those limiting social influences, you would still be in a male or female body, which surely affects your thinking and emotions, but much less so without all the restrictions. And you would be able to feel the difference. If boys and girls were brought up in a more neutral way, gender itself would not be such a strong influence on your development, especially in regard to your self-image. You are more or less terrorized by images and definitions of femininity and masculinity that make you feel extremely normative and come with value judgements that do not logically make sense when projected onto the biological reality of the body.

What is the difference between men and women if you were to remove those environmental influences, if there were a gender-neutral upbringing?

The uniqueness within each person would have much more space to thrive. This would be noticeable in how society sees you. You would be less defined by your body, which is of course as it should be. It is strange that as a person, a human, and a soul, society defines you by your body, your gender. This judgement turns everything upside down. It is the outgrowth of a simplistic, materialistic worldview that regards physical reality as the only real thing and everything else, especially your emotional life and consciousness as "subjective" and therefore less real or relevant.

The truth is that all physical matter, everything you see and perceive with your eyes and other senses has its origin in something beyond the material. You can call this something "spiritual," or "God," or the "soul," or the "Unnamable." The fact is that everything that exists in space and time, for example, your mortal body, and the world around you, emanates from a creative source that is outside of time and space, outside of this three-dimensional reality. The real you IS this source.

Everything you perceive with your physical senses is a fraction of a much greater reality. If you consider this temporary fraction to be the only thing there is and see yourself as a mortal body with either male or female characteristics, and hang your whole identity on that, you impoverish your life immensely. You ignore the complex inner reality that exists within you, and you misunderstand the infinite depth of who you are as a soul—a divine spark that can clothe itself in all kinds of forms, bodies, and identities.

If children were raised in a more gender-neutral way sexuality would become less of a taboo. That does not necessarily mean "anything goes." But it does mean that one's sexuality would no longer be branded as base and sinful, as if the need for it is something to be ashamed of. Men and women have become alienated from their sexual nature in an unnatural way. Sexuality was considered at most a necessary evil by many religions and people caught up in these belief systems were forbidden to explore their sexual feelings in a joyful, open way.

In truth, sexuality can potentially open up a space for love, intimacy and pleasure that enables people to connect at a very deep level. In a mature society, sexuality would be understood as an expression of love between people who use their bodies as channels. Reproduction would be seen as an option, as one outcome of sexuality, but not the most essential. Sexuality would be regarded primarily as union, not of two bodies, but of two souls. There would be less focus on the outside, and more on the inside. The body would then be regarded as an extension of or an emanation from the soul, the soul that dances in matter. The soul being recognized as the most essential.

The difference between male and female then becomes less dominant. Every person has masculine and feminine qualities. Every human being is a soul at their core.

Yes, indeed. It would be best to detach any labels whatsoever when referring to masculinity and femininity.

But you did speak just now in a more universal, metaphysical sense of the masculine as the one-pointed focus that makes individuality possible, and the feminine as the oceanic oneness that connects everything.

Certainly. Day and night are real, as is sick and healthy, young, and old. These polarities exist. The point is not to hang your identity on them. Don't believe you have to behave a certain way because you're a man or think it can't be any other way because you're a woman. That kind of thinking blocks the outflow of your soul. Your soul has masculine and feminine aspects and needs both to fully express itself.

Now we arrive at the third point. I'll repeat what I summarized earlier. It is important to realize that the original masculine and feminine energy are inextricably linked, because this has enormous consequences on how we imagine God, understand ourselves as a soul that carries both aspects, and finally, how we function as a man or woman. If we understand this, then we can distinguish between original masculinity and femininity on the one hand, and destructive, ego-based femininity and masculinity on the other. Can you elaborate on the third point, which is how we function as man or woman?

I will, but I'm going to devote a separate chapter to that. The next chapter will be about how you currently function as a man or woman. I will particularly focus on how men are wounded as a result of the restrictive expectations and prescriptions that are placed upon them.

This is a global problem.

In the following chapter, I will distinguish between original or heart-based masculinity and femininity on the one hand, and ego-based masculinity and femininity on the other.

Chapter 6- The wounded male

In this chapter you discuss how the male loses himself, his soul, and his freedom to be an individual because of the limiting concept of masculinity.

The purpose of this chapter is to point out the serious distortion that exists within the psyches of men and women. Men who are unaware and unable to incorporate the feminine aspect of their souls become trapped in a one-sided, impoverished understanding of themselves. And women who do not embrace their own masculine energy are weakened and unable to sufficiently direct their own lives.

What happens to a man who gradually suppresses his own feminine energy?

Men suppress their emotions because to reveal them would indicate weakness. Emotions make you vulnerable. When an emotion comes over you and shakes you up, you can feel naked and out of control for a period of time, but to be moved in this way is the essence of being human. If you block your emotions and don't allow yourself to feel them, you resist the flow of life. To live, you must feel your emotions. They go together.

When you allow your emotions to move through, you grow, you're more aware of what is alive inside you—your thoughts, feelings, judgments, and desires. If you suppress your natural human ability to be moved and affected by your emotions, you interrupt the flow of your life, which affects the growth of your consciousness. Your mind loses flexibility and becomes rigid, you seek security and control, your ability to cry and laugh exuberantly is also lost, and you become emotionally numb.

Is emotional numbness—being disconnected from your feelings—the essence of the male wound?

Emotional numbness is another way of saying you are cast out of your heart. When you are forbidden to feel your emotions, you lose contact with your soul. The heart is the gateway to the soul and the energetic wound in men is located in the area of the heart.

You mentioned that both sexes are negatively affected by social conditioning and the denial of the original unity of masculine and feminine energy in every human being. How does a woman weaken herself by not using her masculine energy?

When women reject their own masculine energy, they deprive themselves of their freedom and creative power. They will try to fit in, avoid conflict, and won't dare stand out or be original.

It is a feminine trait to want to keep things harmonious. It is part of the conditioned feminine energy to be empathetic and malleable.

Yes, although men can have that tendency too because they also have a conditioned feminine side. Humans are an interplay of conditioned male and female energies. But the tendency not to express your own unique truth and safely blend in with the group is indeed the result of a distorted feminine energy. This energy artificially maintains unity but at the expense of being trapped. It does "what one ought to do," and what is considered "right."

What men often do when they swallow their truth for an extended period of time due to an intolerant environment that forces them to do so, is to become passively or overtly aggressive. They manifest aggression by demonstrating rude, hurtful, and insensitive behavior. They also exhibit it by being emotionally absent or operating on autopilot—doing what is asked of them without truly agreeing to it.

You can witness this in their relationships and how they are in their work environments. Men aren't really there, they perform their tasks in a dull, machine-like way. They are not in touch with their inner freedom. They might try to find it when they are alone, or away from their job, but it doesn't work or help because whatever they do— exercise, drink, hang out with friends— it won't relieve the pain of self-denial. If anything is going to change and happen anew, men must face their feelings directly and understand them consciously rather than numb themselves.

And women? What do they do when they swallow their truth?

Women tend to deny themselves for a longer period of time than men. Men flare up and act aggressively in reaction to self-denial, but it is not a lasting solution and can become its own problem. For women, self-denial can be taken to such an extreme that they completely forget about themselves, seriously neglect their needs, and can remain trapped for years in relationships or an environment that draws them away from their creativity and autonomy.

A latent dissatisfaction and sense of rebellion is palpable in men who operate on autopilot and hobble along uninspired by what they are doing. Women are more likely to ignore those kinds of emotions out of learned docility and instead of rebelling or feeling angry they are more prone to lethargy, fatigue, psychosomatic disorders, or depression.

You say self-denial in men is more likely to lead to aggression. Can you explain that?

It is more precise to say that to deny one's own individuality in regard to masculine energy tends to lead to rebellion. This can happen in men and women. Every person has their own mix of masculine and feminine energy. Generally speaking, men are more familiar with the masculine energy in themselves than the feminine, and are more likely to be aggressive, while women are more prone to depression.

Of course, there are individual differences. For example, there are sensitive men who naturally feel at home with their feminine energy, but who also experience the downside—lack of boundaries, indecisiveness, and losing themselves in relationships due to lack of self-awareness. These men may be more susceptible to symptoms found on the depressive spectrum.

But when a man's masculine energy erupts into aggression, an unreasonable and out of control defensiveness arises, which is pure aggression. He feels out of focus, destructive and wants to free himself from the oppressive bonds that imprison him caused by feelings of resistance that have been long suppressed and have at last surfaced. Then, you see an angry passion that leaves no room for empathy. In this extreme form, the world is either black or white. Male aggression is problematic in the world at large. This blind aggressiveness in the male personality which flares up is a cry for help. It is damaging to him, others, and the earth.

I'm not speaking about a man's healthy assertiveness that knows how to set boundaries. I'm speaking about a deep anger that comes from misunderstood pain, and which is a blind attempt to solve that pain. However, when a man expresses his anger in this way, it does not soothe the pain. The exact opposite happens. This kind of aggression destroys the world.

You are saying that this aggressive masculine energy is not only a personal problem but can also be understood as a threat on a global level.

Yes. It is crucial to understand the origins of this aggression and not fall into simplistic discussions about "what men are really like." This aggression is destructive on a large scale, and it can take extreme forms including political violence, blind violence against women, and the exploitation of nature.

I feel it, and I'm scared. I get a deep sense of suffocation that presses on my heart.

This is what happens, the heart is suppressed by this kind of masculine energy, and it leads to indescribable pain and confusion in the male psyche. When there is no awareness of what is going on, these feelings turn into destructive rage. Throughout history men have been forbidden to connect with their hearts, their feelings. Young men are maimed internally when raised in a society that believes in these extremely restrictive and harsh definitions of masculinity. They grow to up believe they must swallow their intuitive sense of truth, work hard, protect the weak—women, children, community—and distinguish themselves by achieving and being successful.

Inwardly, men were forced to suppress their vulnerability; be strong and never cry, be tough, not sensitive. They were to model the kind of authority figure who points the way or become the authority figure themselves and impose their will on others. There was no room for the originality and creativity of the male energy that resided in the heart. This yoke has broken men's hearts. They live with a broken, closed heart. This is the tight feeling you felt in your heart when you tuned into the wounded male energy.

I feel cut off from life, from what is vibrant and flowing. It is like I'm not allowed to let an essential part of myself flourish. I have to surrender, to obey and be of service to something greater that emanates nothing positive, only coercion, duty, fear. The highest achievement is to meet the outside world's expectations and receive approval for it. However, this approval comes for being an obedient, well-adjusted man, not for who you really are. To bear this pain of self-denial, you must harden, protect your heart, and keep your feelings at bay. Opening your heart is dangerous because you could lose control, stop functioning, and lose your sense of self-respect and autonomy.

You are now channeling "the forbidden male." What else do you feel?

That I, as the forbidden male, should limit my sexuality to that of lust and be careful about opening my heart in relationships or during sexual contact because it is so threatening. When I open my heart, I'm gone, there's nothing left of me. I have to restrain myself, not open myself too much. I need protection, because if I reveal my full vulnerability there is no one or nothing to protect me. Then I am defenseless.

"What do you need,"' I ask the forbidden male. The answer I receive is "that someone sees me."

What wants to be seen is the heart, the soul, the unique individuality.

I also feel something about that anger, the aggression that arises as a result of the oppression of one's own soul. It is a survival instinct or drive for revenge that eventually kicks in because of self-denial. If you feel oppressed in this way for long enough, you want to reclaim your identity but in the wrong way. You want to turn the tables and exercise control and dominate something or someone yourself, to feel that "it is yours," and get satisfaction from it. Out of powerlessness you exercise power over nature, life, the world around you. Because life has been denied to you, you want to control it in a mental way. This is happening globally through technology, science, and commerce. Traditionally, religious dogma, political wars and conflicts exercised this kind of control and power.

Pain precedes anger and the compulsion to control. When you don't feel seen and accepted as you naturally are, when your unique self is pushed out and you have to conform to prevailing mores, you become emotionally wounded and disfigured. The wounded man will then convert the pain he experiences into anger or frustration, which manifests in the urge to control.

It is important to understand why anger is the preferred response in men. This emotion actually fits best with the prevailing cultural mores that consider it more manly to be angry than to be sad. Anger in the form of ideological enthusiasm, authoritarian behavior or even oppression of others is not taboo for many people. Traditional notions of masculinity condone it.

Both men and women feel this pain, and when it becomes unbearable, you will turn it into something that seems manageable to you. For men, it is aggression and dominance since the distorted self seeks possibilities within the prevailing mores, that is, within the prevailing definitions of masculinity.

The distorted wounded self in its unconscious, locked-up state, has no idea of alternatives. It has surrendered to a limiting self-image and the existing doctrines. The traditional rules in society allow a man to be aggressive. This counts as being decisive, a leader, a charismatic quality in political leaders. Think of dictators who won the admiration and support of the popular masses with extremely aggressive ideologies.

Although the excesses of aggression are in general condemned by the established order, many forms of male dominance and authoritarian behavior have long been considered to be okay. The anger that smolders in the collective male energy is tolerated and even approved of by the establishment, although that anger is actually an unconscious reaction directed against the establishment.

And this anger also threatens the established order, if you think of terrorism, aggressive corporate profit making, environmental pollution and wars waged for nationalistic or religious motives.

It is a paradox. The established order consists of old-fashioned, masculine dominant energy, and at the same time that order claims to fight against aggression in the form of terrorism or dictatorial regimes. But what is the established order itself based on? Is there really a heart-based energy in it, a sincere pursuit of tolerance, mutual understanding, protection of the individual and a fair distribution of resources? There is much talk about democratic ideas and human rights, but in practice, those in power who are not concerned about the values of equality, justice, and protection of the weak, including nature, rule the world.

The mighty of the earth are wounded, deformed men themselves?

Sure, with a few exceptions.

You can speak of a vicious circle. The traditional definition of masculinity suppresses a man's soul, and the pain caused by it leads to rage and a desire for control that does not really break through this distortion, but in a way reinforces it.

It's a profound problem. The only possibility for real transformation is to break through one-sided, mutilating ideas about masculinity and femininity. Men are in a collective prison that suffocates their souls. They can start kicking against the walls and bars, but that won't get them out. They must understand the nature of the prison and rise above it with inner strength. That prison is not material, but spiritual; not something on the outside, but something on the inside. Liberation comes from within, and you don't achieve it together with others, but alone. By that I mean, it requires an individual choice. When you inwardly decide to let go of prevailing mores and limiting beliefs about masculinity, you come into living contact with your soul and step outside of humanity's collective heritage. You leave prison through individual self-liberation.

Letting go of the traditional image of masculinity requires a man to detach himself from the prevailing social order?

Men are required to see the extent to which they have been manipulated. First of all, this must be an inner, emotional step. Because they have been cast out of their emotional life, they think mechanistically. "Getting out" doesn't necessarily mean "doing something" such as quitting your job or going on a backpacking trip. That's not the solution. It is more subtle than that. The situation begs for reflection and a renewal of contact with your soul, with your feelings.

As soon as you experience displeasure or feel suffocated or oppressed in your life, you are inclined to ask, "what should I do?" You look for answers in specific actions—quit my job, break up my relationship, renovate my house, go on a retreat! The question "What should I do?" is a manifestation of the underlying problem. An action-oriented way of thinking is a sign that the masculine energy has gone crazy because it seeks solutions on the level of "doing."

This tendency is everywhere. On the global level, there is a constant search for external solutions, solutions at the level of doing, acting, and directing. For example, the environment—how do we control pollution in such a way that it decreases? Figures, calculations, and modern technologies bring the possibility of a solution into sight. But the tendency to calculate and solve the problem through doing and action completely fails. Ultimately, nothing changes.

The only solution is a change of consciousness, a return to the soul, the necessity to restore contact with your inner world, your feelings, your passion, your living core. What is missing is the lack of contact with the soul. This is the real problem for the individual and across the globe. The entire world is caught in an unhinged, destructive masculine energy and men suffer from it as much as women. However, they suffer unconsciously. The first step to healing is to become aware.

To return to the framework you outlined in Chapter 5, we distinguished three points, of which you have now explained the third. I will summarize.

It is important to realize that the original male and female energies are one in a complementary sense, because this has enormous consequences for (1) how we imagine God, (2) understand ourselves as a soul that carries both aspects, and finally, (3) how we function as a man or woman.

With regard to the third point, you have shown us that the impoverished definition of masculinity as hard, tough, controlling and emotionally numb has extremely destructive consequences, such as large-scale aggression and intense psychological suffering in men.

You indicated that if we understand this, we can then distinguish between original masculinity and femininity on the one hand and ego-based destructive masculinity and femininity on the other.

In the next chapter, I will discuss the difference between the original and the destructive masculine energy. Understanding the difference is crucial for women, not only because they are in constant relationship with men, but also because it is important for them to recognize and integrate within themselves their own original masculine energy.

Chapter 7- Destructive versus original masculine energy

To become aware of how your belief in a harsh, wounding image of masculinity limits you, it is important to realize that there is a different, more mature, and liberating image of masculinity you can take on.

If you don't know you're in a prison, you can't get out.

In the West, people have started to think differently about masculinity. The stereotypical macho version is made fun of, and now men are allowed and even expected to be sensitive.

Look at the political leaders of most countries, the CEOs of large corporations, or rulers in general. They are still quite macho.

Yes, that is true. So, the old image is still dominant?

In most of the world, yes. I would like to distinguish between this limited type of masculinity, which I call destructive, and what I call primordial masculine energy.

What is primordial masculine energy?

It is the energy of individuality. In chapters five and six, I described the interactions between a male and female who are on the soul level. The feminine represents the One, the connector, the oceanic. The masculine brings in the Manifold, variety, autonomy, selfhood, and individuality. Together, these polar energies create the dance of creation.

For example, as a human being you are able to intensely empathize with another, which is a feminine quality. Through empathy you feel a oneness. At the same time, you are able to act, choose and stand in the world as a separate individual. You have your own inner world. You can share something essential about yourself, your deep feelings, and connect with them and at the same time remain an independent, creative consciousness with your own free will. Thus, as a human being you are female and male at the same time.

So, masculine energy in its original form is the energy of individuality and separateness in the sense of autonomy and self-sufficiency.

Yes, the original masculine energy in constant equilibrium with the original feminine energy is balanced and mature. Conflict does not enter into it, only an organic cooperation.

Think of a conversation you have with a friend, for example, part of it consists of listening and empathizing with the other person, which is essential for communication. On the other hand, you offer your own experiences and point of view. Good communication always consists of an alternation between feminine and masculine qualities. To connect with the other person and be open to their perspective (feminine), while also staying tuned to your feelings and expressing your perspective (masculine). "I understand what you feel and think…let me tell you what I feel and think." This back and forth is natural or should be natural.

Wherever you find original masculine energy, it will always be connected to and interact with original feminine energy, and vice versa. That is true by definition.

The significant difference between the original and the destructive male energy is that the latter opposes the female energy and engages in battle with it. This also applies to destructive feminine energy when it has lost connection with the original masculine energy and becomes boundless, chaotic, manipulative, and suffocating. When the two disconnect from each other, both energies become destructive and at that moment duality comes into play making rigid what was originally fluid.

When a person's male and female energy gets separated, something in them is killed. When they function according to the caricatures of masculinity and femininity that your tradition dictates, men become mechanical, flat, and dead inside. They are cut off from their liveliness, their feelings, and the natural flow of emotions that is part of being human. You mutilate their inner life when you force boys into the straitjacket of "being a good, strong man."

The destructive aspect of the masculine energy is a creation, a construct. Isn't their "natural competitive nature" aggressive and dominant?

Men are not aggressive by nature. That is a fabrication. Aggression is not natural at all. In a mature society, aggression is a sign that something has gone off the rails, that an aberration has occurred. It can take place in both women and men. A normal human emotion such as fear or fright, if suppressed, can turn into anger and resentment.

For example, if you are forced to do something new that you're afraid to do by an outside authority, you might feel resistant and angry. When your boundaries have been violated like that, the pain and powerlessness you feel inside, which is ignored by those around you, can turn into a permanent mistrust of others. In the long run, you might always feel guarded or defensive, feeling you have to defend, protect, or shield yourself from other people and this can lead to aggression. Your feelings are locked up tight, all spontaneity is lost, and you feel increasingly frustrated. Often, an empty, flat feeling lingers, but at some point, it will express itself as aggression and even manifest explosively as resentment and anger. This kind of aggression builds up slowly and is not inherent in "the male nature." It is the result of a severely dysfunctional social conditioning that discourages people in general and men in particular from staying in touch with their emotions and feelings.

You say that aggression is not natural, but it occurs in the animal kingdom, doesn't it? I'm thinking of an animal's territorial instincts.

You cannot compare the animal kingdom to the human kingdom. I know it's fashionable these days to say that man is "actually an animal" with a bit more brain capacity, but man comes into the world from a completely different dimension of consciousness. Emotions in animals exist, but they have no ability to process or reflect on them. This is what charms people about animals.

You feel the innocence and purity in animal behavior even when it is derailed, because you know the animal can't help it. The animal is so pure, people say. But purity is not a lofty moral quality if you cannot be otherwise. It is not a real choice for an animal to be "pure." It is not an achievement. You can admire that quality in animals, but human consciousness is in a different dimension. The human being has self-awareness and individual choice, the animal does not. The purity you should strive for is not that of unconscious animality, but of an open awareness, being in touch with the soul, able to understand and maturely manage emotions of fear and anger.

Yes, aggression in animals exists, but it is often short-lived rising and falling away in a single moment. The dog that barks and growls at you in the street is, as it were, saying, "Go Away!" When you do, the next second the dog is playfully chasing a squirrel without a second thought of you. There is no continuous, smoldering, frustrated deadness in the dog's aggression that is so characteristic of the state of consciousness in aggressive males.

In my previous book, The Forbidden Female Speaks, *I addressed the wounds in the female psyche caused by past conditioning. Women carry a deep feeling of "emptiness in their abdomen," coupled with a lack of self-esteem, which leaves them completely unaware of their own strength.*

In the book I briefly mention that men are more likely to suffer from a wound of the heart, cut off from their feelings. Is this also the hallmark of destructive masculine energy? Men are forbidden to connect to their own hearts, forced to prove they are tough, strong, and powerful? They feel they have to do this to meet the demands and expectations of the culture they grew up in. This has systematically happened to them. Is there a cumulative, collective, and destructive masculine energy that profoundly affects our lives, individually and globally?

Yes, that's right. I would say the essential characteristic of destructive male energy is that it is not connected to the female energy. Men who are not in touch with their own feminine energy, the feminine aspect of their soul, are deeply wounded. It is a psychological injury, which you can recognize in the following symptoms.

- Inability to recognize their feelings
- Inability to express their feelings properly
- Mentally preoccupied—"in their heads"
- A lack of connection with their own body

I recognize this from my own observations of men. It seems that suppressing one's feelings and emotional spontaneity leads to a mechanical, flat, dead feeling inside. This can create an inner emptiness that leads to depression, feelings of meaninglessness, feeling closed or cut off, a sense of isolation and alienation, which is unbearable and eventually must be "acted out." The pain can turn into uncontrolled anger or frustration, which is not liberating, and reinforces feelings of isolation. It is from that state of being cut off that a charged attitude arises towards "the female."

What do you feel?

The female represents what the wounded man had to reject in himself, his sensitivity, his liveliness. This creates ambiguous feelings in him in relation to women. I feel that in extreme variants this can lead, on the one hand, to misogyny ("I hate you because you are what I am not allowed to be") and, on the other hand, to addiction, and an excessive dependence on women, or specifically the female partner.

Yes, men love women but if they are denied their own feminine, sensitive side, then in the outside world they will view women as "the other," as beings who are completely different from themselves. This is incorrect and leads to an imbalance. The original masculine energy is not alienated from the feminine but is naturally connected to it. A man who feels at home in his heart, who allows himself to be tender and dares to express himself can connect with a woman much more easily than a man who has to hide his feelings all the time, who has to restrain himself because he lives behind a mask acting "strong and tough." It is characteristic of the destructive masculine energy to see the woman or the feminine as "the other" and "the incomprehensible."

This leads to a contradictory attitude towards women, which you characterized above as a love-hate relationship. I would put it this way, men who possess destructive masculine energy are afraid of women, and don't know how to behave towards them. On the one hand, they are emotionally dependent on them, having lost touch with their own feminine side. On the other hand, the prevailing expectation of a man requires him never to be emotionally dependent on anyone, and preferably to have no emotional needs at all.

This creates a split in the male psyche, which causes widespread misery in the world. If you are not allowed to be vulnerable and emotionally dependent, and habitually have to suppress your feelings, you become rigid inside. You will develop hollow ideologies that give you something to hold on to but in fact, you are walking in the desert. You deny your need for water, use your will and perseverance to move on, but it is all in vain. You yearn for the oasis of feminine energy. You yearn to feel like a human being.

The average man's emotions have been amputated but he doesn't realize it. To the extent that he does not realize it, he will not understand why he is suffering and will develop a fear of, or even an aversion to, women. They provoke him, because they show him what he lacks by being who they are, and that makes him feel vulnerable. He can do two things in that unconscious state, become dismissive and closed, or become possessive and jealous.

Both of these fear-based responses are aggressive in nature—he rejects the feminine and keeps it at bay or wants to capture and dominate it. Both responses are all about control. Control is opposed to feeling. The biggest taboo the male faces is the taboo of feeling his feelings—except for the expression of anger, rage, and aggression.

What to do?

Men have to change. The mantle of traditional masculine traits that men have taken on is instinctive, and deeply ingrained. That is the problem and women have come to accept it. A man is masculine if he is closed and tough, weak if he is sensitive. That's the stereotypical image and women unconsciously adhere to it. They may think they want men to be different, want a man to be lively, vulnerable, and open, but unconsciously they cling to the idea of him as an anchor, a rock—silent, strong, tough.

Women are conflicted about what kind of masculinity is attractive to them because they have not let go of the old image of femininity, which is to be caring, loving, and vulnerable. The sweet, adaptable woman needs a powerful, dominant man. Two halves complimenting each other is not only outdated, but also false and limiting. Nevertheless, it has great romantic appeal.

There is a deep desire in the unconscious human being to merge with something greater. The male-female polarity has an enormous appeal and is a source of endless fantasies, imagery, and reveries.

Is that all fake?

There is no room for individuality in the image of two halves making each other whole—that is the biggest miss.

Realize that at your core you are a soul, not a human being. Your humanity is a form you have temporarily assumed. The human form is gender-based, you are male or female. But that's just your form. You as a man or woman are only a form. Realize that you are a unique soul.

What makes you you—what makes you unique is not your masculinity or femininity.

You can do these simple exercises.

- Imagine you are a tree.
- Imagine you are a mountain.
- Imagine that you are a woman if you are now a man and imagine that you are a man if you are now in a female body.

Do these three exercises with full attention. Feel how you can imagine being these life forms while at the same time remaining you. You are still you while you observe and experience trying on these different forms.

In fact, this exercise is not a mere play of the imagination. You have been a tree, a mountain, a man, and a woman in other lifetimes. Your consciousness is more expanded and grander than you think. It can and wants to express and develop itself in many, endless forms, not just the human form. Do you realize how creative your original consciousness is?

If you allow your individuality, who you are, to be defined by human definitions of masculinity or femininity, you put yourself in a prison, and it will oppress you terribly, especially as your awareness of yourself as an individual, a unique soul, starts to grow.

The first step to self-liberation for men and women is to let go of the idea that you are essentially a man or a woman. You are essentially you, a soul who is unique and cannot be contained in one form.

It is clear to me now how destructive masculine energy differs from original or mature masculine energy. I wonder how this distinction applies to feminine energy. I have described the destructive version of the feminine energy in The Forbidden Female Speaks. I would like to know how the destructive masculine and feminine energy interact. Does the aggressive, dominant male energy need a weak, submissive female energy opposite it?

Submissive feminine and dominant masculine energy are linked together in an unstable way. They seem to be complementary, but they are in fact adversarial. The destructive masculine energy negates the intrinsic dignity of the feminine energy. In the background, in secret, so to speak, "he" cannot do without her, which is why he wants to control her. He wants to possess her through coercion and control. The destructive male energy is violent, driven by restless anger and frustration. He is out of touch with his own soul and cannot relate to the feminine, both inside and outside himself in a healthy manner. If she goes along with it, the feminine energy ends up at the other extreme, she is in denial, and has lost her own, autonomous power.

What is feminine autonomy about? Why does the dominant or destructive male want to possess something dead? It rules out any meaningful interaction, is that right?

The autonomous power of the feminine energy is to connect and give life, not merely biologically, but psychologically—it inspires, creates from the heart, and reaches out. The heart-based feminine energy lifts one up to a level of love and oneness where the soul—your unique core—can create and thrive. The feminine energy connects you to the heart, the source of life, and that is precisely the place the lower masculine energy wants to stay away from. Opening the heart equates with giving up your defenses and need for control. The destructive masculine energy is opposed to life itself. It is toxic and deeply resents the higher feminine. When women accept the negative images of femininity that they have been fed, it is evident they do not fully appreciate themselves and will tolerate abuse without being aware they are.

The original or higher feminine energy, which approaches the other from an open heart, challenges the destructive, lower masculine energy.

Something in him is inexorably attracted to her, for even the most defensive, self-contained creatures cannot escape the call of truth, and love is truth.

But if the male ego has to lay down its arms, open up to the truth, and acknowledge the fear that drives him, a fight or flight response may occur. The disruptive power of love can be so overwhelming and threatening that the male ego wants to protect himself at all costs, either by fleeing or by fighting, that is, accepting only the non-threatening aspect of the feminine energy, not the challenging one.

This is the answer to your question of why the lower male ego wants to possess a dead thing— the submissive, caring, well-adapted woman is not threatening to him. He doesn't have to change. He can still draw his life force from her. The man is not really alive, he is mechanical and emotionally impoverished as a result of denying his own feminine energy. He is attracted to women for their vibrant, emotional nature. He feels himself coming alive through them, but because of his inherent compulsion to control, he will also want to curtail and restrict their aliveness. This leads to a tug of war within the so-called "relationship." But there is no genuine relationship here because meaningful interaction requires the presence of love and freedom.

Such a power-driven relationship will break down sooner or later, because the more dead and submissive the woman becomes, the less the man will care about her, and he will eventually neglect or reject her. The more alive she becomes, and therefore autonomous and independent, the more it will arouse his fear and therefore his aggression. He will hinder her through jealous, controlling behavior. Then she either rebels and leaves, or she gives in and languishes. There is no natural equilibrium in this dynamic. The relationship is unstable by definition.

Women can be drawn to the lower masculine energy in an almost perverse way. No woman consciously wants to be submissive or controlled, yet we can be attracted to a certain toughness, roughness, even callousness in a man, qualities we associate with strength and leadership.

The image of the "real man" as supremely tough and unyielding is deeply rooted in the human imagination in both men and women. The real man who is "made of stone," the unwavering leader who "puts affairs in order," the male authority with near divine authority—this image (from which the notion of God as a male deity is derived), is born of fear. Behind it is a deep, existential fear of life in all its capriciousness and unpredictability. This fear creates the need for an outside authority.

The ensuing image of tough masculinity is a life-threatening image, because the harsh, unyielding toughness of the lower masculine energy only offers solace to people who do not want to think, feel, act, and decide for themselves. This lower masculine energy thrives on making people feel docile. You can see its strong influence in politics. Think of the typical image of a political leader, or a boss or CEO. It is the ideal of the man with an iron fist who takes the lead and "cuts the knot." This type of man does exist.

There is a strong emphasis on decisiveness and control. It is less about content and more about form. This kind of leadership is based on "having everything under control," whereas the reality is usually quite different. Such a leader often shows paranoid or even psychotic traits. They create chaos and oppression, because they ignore facts that do not suit them, refuse to be flexible, engage in real communication, and allow different perspectives. Their lack of empathy goes hand in hand with (extreme) cruelty and they crush anything truly innovative. This traditional male, fear-based leadership is always conservative and defensive.

This same dynamic occurs in a love relationship when the masculine energy is out of touch with the feminine, is rigid and mechanical, and wants to dominate as an end in itself. Only women who are out of touch with their own original masculine energy will initially feel attracted to this "hard" masculinity. This kind of attraction comes from an inner emptiness, a lack of self-awareness, and the need for an outside authority. But sooner or later, the woman will fall out of love, because the unhealthy power dynamic mentioned before will convince her that this lower male energy will never fulfill her needs.

What are the main consequences for the male psyche in regard to this age old ideal of "tough masculinity?"

It has caused extensive psychological damage. Their inability to feel has been impaired and to feel is to live. Emotional numbness has grave consequences, reduced connection with the body, an overly active mind focused on solving problems and a lack of feeling grounded. Because thinking is disconnected from intuition, which comes from the heart, men are locked up in their heads. They are supposed to be leaders and protectors, but they feel burdened by a responsibility that is too great for them to carry. Their duties and responsibilities crush the lively inner child in them, and give rise to pent-up frustration, and a complicated mixture of guilt and rage.

The main problem is that men lose the connection with their living core, their soul. The same goes for women whose creative power and independence are suppressed. They also lose touch with their soul. Both men and women are damaged by the traditional cages they are put in, because their individuality is disregarded. For some, it leads to aggression and a lack of compassion, for others it leads to passivity and depression. Both sexes suffer. The unique soul of the individual human being is pushed into the background.

What to do?

Recognition of the problem is a prerequisite. As long as you believe in the dualistic images of masculinity and femininity, you remain brainwashed and will be unhappy without understanding why.

There has been a lot of criticism of the traditional definitions regarding masculinity and femininity. For roughly a century, women's equality has been increasingly recognized in many respects, at least on paper. It seems to me that especially in the West, men are more aware of their feelings and increasingly allowed and encouraged to express them. In some circles it has even become a "must." Men are scolded for being insensitive and emotionally closed. Old fashioned male authoritarian behavior is considered unattractive. Sometimes, I get the impression that masculinity is considered suspect tout court. Men need to become more feminine. It seems that in feminist and in spiritual circles, femininity is considered to be morally superior.

Men do not need to become more feminine, they need to embrace their original masculine energy, which naturally connects them with their higher (heart-based) feminine energy. To portray the feminine as "good," morally superior, more humane and loving, and the masculine as "bad" or intrinsically aggressive and insensitive is to create a false duality. It is important to realize that feminine energy can also be destructive when it is fear or ego-based, and second, that there is a higher heart-based masculine energy that needs to be liberated in every human being. The qualities of original masculine energy are discernment, focus, self-awareness, truthfulness, and independence.

The original masculine energy is intrinsically motivated to explore the new and "break the rules," especially rules built on power-based authority. Think about the archetypical image of the naughty young boy who provokes his parents and is bent on doing things his own way. There is something of a rule-breaking adventurousness in the original male energy, and this is a creative and vital aspect of higher masculinity. It is present in both boys and girls. It is a soul attribute. This attribute can be smothered by an imperious or possessive female energy that wants to tame and contain this "boyish" love of freedom and playfulness. The woman with destructive or disempowered feminine energy experiences an emptiness within her and seeks to lean on or claim the life force inside the masculine. The unhealthy feminine seeks to conquer the male through psychological manipulation—acting helpless and playing on their feelings of guilt and responsibility, thus controlling the male energy, and keeping it "on a leash."

If we recognize that both male and female energy have a higher and a lower, or an original and a destructive version, then we can approach the subject of "masculinity" in a more subtle and truthful way?

Yes, the male wound can only be healed if the wound is recognized. Men have been cut off not only from "feminine qualities" such as empathy and tenderness, but also from "masculine qualities" such as adventurousness, originality, truthfulness, and the healthy tendency to dethrone false authorities.

In other words, healing the wound in men is not just about reconnecting with their feminine energy, but also feeling at home with their own original masculine energy. That's the forbidden male.

That's right, and it is what I want to talk about now. How does a man regain access to his heart and reconnect with his soul, instead of staying trapped in a socially constructed role? How can he find his way back to both his original masculine and feminine energy?

Chapter 8- Healing the male wound

We have discussed and diagnosed the male wound. Throughout history, men have been forced to suppress their feminine energy—their feelings, emotions, and intuition—and disconnect from their original masculine energy, the higher or heart-based, masculine qualities of self-awareness, truthfulness, discernment, and adventurousness.

The suppression of both energies has been emotionally scarring and has caused a wound in the hearts of men. How can men heal this inner wound?

First, let us take a step back. The greatest wound inflicted on men has been the severance of natural communication with their own soul. The same has happened in a unique way for women. Stereotypically defining masculinity and femininity and organizing society along those lines has caused untold suffering. In both cases, whether you are male or female, you were discouraged from experiencing your own wholeness, your wholeness as a human being, as an individual, and as a soul.

But think for a moment about who benefits from this? If you force people into believing in duality, and fixed societal identities, you suppress their individual freedom. You design a moral framework which prescribes how people must behave; if they obey, they are good, if they deviate, they are bad. That's how you control people.

Who devised and applied those frameworks? Who wanted to control people in this way?

Many religious and political institutions/organizations embody the energy of power and control. Political and religious leaders are averse to free individual expression; indeed, they thrive on dulling the human mind and spirit.

Human history consistently shows that people have a psychological hunger for power and control and on a large scale it leads to wars, and within societies it creates brutal competition in the workplace and in the distribution of money and goods. On a micro level there is the everyday exertion of control in parent-child relations, marriages, and friendships. When you see women and men who are restricted from expressing their unique selves, you will see them manifest a hunger for power and control.

Contact with the soul brings awareness to a person's inner strength, wisdom, and their independence from worldly powers. That is exactly why these powers, including most religions, do not want people to stray from the beaten track, much less live authentically—in touch with their own truth and creative inspiration.

The essential question is what exactly is this hunger for power that leads them away from contact with their own soul and makes them want to control people, and life in general? Instead of discussing specific ways power is abused, past or present, and identifying particular "culprits," I prefer to focus on the universal, psychological energy behind the need for power. That's the crux of the matter.

What is that destructive hunger for power and control, which among other things, caused the male wound, and where does it come from?

To rephrase your question without pointing out "bad forces" or playing the victim-offender game, you might ask yourself, what in me wants to exert that power? Where do I judge, label, create moral boxes of good and bad and force myself and others to conform?

Aha...you are saying that the culprit, the controlling ego, the power abuser is within us?

Where else?

I get it. If we blame the evil doer outside ourselves, who caused the wound inside us, like the Church or a political regime or some demonic force, we create the duality of good/ bad, victim/offender, and turn it into a battle with evil doers outside ourselves.

Yes, and then you focus on the proverbial speck of sawdust in the other person's eye, while not seeing the plank in your own eye.

Quoting the Bible: "Why do you look at the speck of sawdust in your brother's eye and pay no attention to the plank in your own eye? How can you say to your brother, "Let me take the speck out of your eye," when all the time there is a plank in your own eye? You hypocrite, first take the plank out of your own eye, and then you will see clearly to remove the speck from your brother's eye."

All true teachers say to look inside to identify what harms us and keeps us from the truth.

It is popular within spiritual circles to point out conspiracies and evildoers that need to be exposed. It seems as if the spiritual quest has turned into a political battle, where the seeker unmasks evil and abusers of power, but most of the time does not unmask himself.

You can choose to fight this battle, and surely there is a lot to be found in the outside world that is not based on love or truth. But the question is—what really interests you? If you are looking for inner liberation, it is better to focus your attention on your inner demons, on the need for or addiction to power and control within your own psyche.

The question then becomes, what in me (in us) desires to exercise power and control in such a way that I lose touch with my intuition, my soul? It must be something unconscious, because who wants to consciously cut off contact with their own soul?

If I had to answer that question, I would say I am in pain, I feel homesick, and separate from the whole, the source. I feel torn apart from a sacred, safe Home, tossed about in a vast, empty, and incomprehensible universe. When I tune into that, I feel confused, bewildered, and there is an urgency to hold onto something, a need for light, for love, for security.

Yes, this is the primal pain of being thrust into duality, of being born as an individual soul. An individual who is born with an innate freedom and creative power enters the world with huge promise, but at the very moment they break away from Oneness, which is the first step towards self-awareness, there is pain and confusion.

In the first messages I received from you (see the book The Jeshua Channelings) you spoke of "cosmic birth pain." How does that pain turn into a desire for power?

When the soul is born two urges drive it, one aims for unity, maintaining contact with the One, and the other dives into Duality, embracing separation and diversity. The move toward unity is what makes the soul conscious. The move toward duality enriches the soul with experience. The soul can only grow and evolve when both elements are present. The soul needs duality in order to gain experience. Thus, opposition between you and the world, between you and "the other" is necessary. The conscious part of your soul increasingly senses the unity behind all diversity. It is at one with everything, because consciousness is in everything, it is a constant field.

But to gain experience you "pretend" there is a You and an Other. You create a playing field of polarities where you want to live and experience the ultimate goal of merging your growing consciousness with your experiential knowledge. In that marriage, so to speak, of consciousness and experience, you transcend the cosmic birth pain and experience an inner wholeness that is sublime and creative. You have become aware of yourself as God.

The alternating movement between unity and duality is the natural dance of the soul, of the evolving free self. The encounter between the male and female is part of that dance. You are one, you have both masculine and feminine qualities within you. Your soul is not gendered. At the same time, you are also two. You were born in a particular form, you either have a male or a female body, and you are attracted to the Other. You want to experience the play of polarities.

This game could be joyous if you brought an aspect of Consciousness into your experience of duality. Then you would remain aware of the Oneness, of the primal security of which you are a part, while you jump into the deep end. However, during the birthing process of the soul, your consciousness is temporarily obscured.

At first you deeply immerse yourself in the experience of duality. The loss of Oneness is painful, but as a young soul you hardly know what you are missing, for you only become aware of it when you know you've lost it. So, you feel a vague loss of "I don't know what," and because you don't get it, you look for a solution for this emptiness and anxiety on the level of Experience within the playing field of polarity and duality.

What you ultimately need to resolve the pain of separation and the frightening void inside you is the awareness of your unbroken oneness with Life and your wholeness as an individual. But instead, you fill the inner void with things outside of yourself and you do this for quite a long time. You fill it with what you experience as Other than yourself, which can give you security, love, warmth, and reassurance. But you still feel empty, small, insignificant, and continue to look for something greater, something outside of you—a mother or father, an authority, a beloved, a God, in hopes it is the thing that is missing.

That's where it goes wrong.

When you feel something is lacking and feel powerless, the desire for power is born. You find an external source of reassurance and then you seek power over that which gives you a sense of security, fulfillment, or love. You want control.

How does that manifest itself?

First of all, power and control are vastly different from love. What you really long for is love, but from the powerless part of yourself you look for something to hold onto and control. Power gives you a sense of control. Think about it—when you feel powerful, you experience a sense of security, it gives you a temporary "fix." For a while, you are not afraid, nor do you suffer. To achieve this, you exert power over something outside of you, which is valuable, complements you, and "makes you whole." Practically speaking, this could be another human being, a partner or lover, or success in any form; financial prosperity, admiration, recognition, or "being needed by another"—there are myriad ways in which the frightened ego tries to fill the void, always by grasping, struggling, and conquering. In essence, you see the other as a source of nourishment, and you feed yourself on someone else's energy.

When you do this, you maintain duality; you hinder your own development when you look outside yourself. You are not aware that the solution lies within you. By turning into your own pain, you realize wholeness is still there within.

How can men heal themselves? The wounded male who genuinely wants to heal himself releases power. He stops forcing himself into boxes, recognizes and lets go of his own desire for power, security, and control. Instead of feeling victimized by forces outside him, others, women, society, he realizes that he has to let go of his own cravings for power and control. In doing so, he opens the door to freedom.

Freedom allows him space to know himself as an individual being, a soul detached from society with its rigid views, a man who is free to open up to his own soul, and a wealth of feelings inside. He is in touch with his imagination and inspiration. Free—he reclaims his inner world. He finds his way back to his sanctuary, his heart, and is no longer ashamed of his humanness, his sensitivity and vulnerability. It is precisely his ability to feel his feelings deeply and express himself openly that makes him strong and wise. It also allows him to approach women in a balanced way, to see them as unique, fellow human beings—as another, but not as "the Other."

The first step to healing the male wound is for the man to realize that how he judges and looks upon himself is heavily influenced by limiting beliefs based on the need for power and control. The second step is to understand that he exercises that power over himself (out of fear) and therefore, he also has the ability to break free from it.

Yes, to break free from a mental prison, you must realize that you are in prison, and then figure out that it is a delusion, something outside of you. "The others," or society keep you trapped there. The need to live up to other people's expectations is the opposite of being free. If you want to control what people think of you, your "image," you are always tense, never free. A man who feels trapped by society's demands and expectations about being a "real man" tries to control the way people respond to him and in the end damages himself. Thus, he constructs his own mental prison.

Let go of control, let others do and think what they want, and you are free.

That sounds quite easy, but as a human being there is a psychological need to "belong," to be loved and appreciated by your family and peers. It's not easy to release control. It's not easy to risk being rejected, to stand alone.

Look at what happens to you when you bend over backwards to please others, when you deny or lose yourself trying to be someone you are not. I dare say that you do more damage to yourself in this way than if you would jump off the cliff and risk being seen as different or "weird."

I interviewed a number of men in preparation for this book, and some of them said they benefited greatly from being in groups of like-minded men. They said that sharing their emotional pain and hardships with other men in a safe atmosphere made an enormous difference.

The presence of like-minded people who are on the same path and feel seen and recognized is very precious. It is helpful, but the most essential step you have to take as an individual man is to undo your own chains. You do that yourself. No one can do it for you because the oppressor is within!

When you internally let go of your need for control, a new world opens up. The presence of like-minded people, or "way showers," who teach by example can invite and encourage you to do so. However, you are the one in charge, you are free to decide whether to break out of prison or not.

Then it seems to me that insight and courage are crucial. Insight into your own mental shackles, the extent to which you have been programmed to follow and believe a set of norms that do not match your true nature, and the courage to step out of that "matrix."

Courage is born of insight and pain. When you suffer, you long for the suffering to end. The more you desire relief, the greater you thirst for knowledge and insight. Desire is creative, especially when it comes from the soul. You will gain the insight you need, and the burning pain of desire will bring you to a point of choice. The jump into freedom requires courage, but the moment you jump in, it will not feel like a choice, it is more like surrender. If you really see the truth, you take the leap. When you truly realize what freedom is, you become free.

I understand what you mean. What struck me about these men's stories is that they often lacked an inspiring example of heart-based or mature masculinity. When they talked about their fathers, they suffered not just from authoritarian, insensitive masculine energy, but also from fathers who were simply absent, "not there" emotionally or spiritually. The father's energy seemed unavailable and weak or numb, not harsh and domineering.

Whether you had an authoritarian, coercive father, or a weak, emotionally absent father, in both cases you had to deal with a disconnected masculine energy that was insufficiently connected to the heart. Restoring that connection to the heart is pioneering work. Most men have to teach this to themselves and actively seek inspiring teachers, books, or other resources to help them. Usually, the energy of their birth family is hardly inspirational, more often the opposite, and that's why men who break free from the straitjacket of traditional masculinity are truly pioneers.

How can you learn to feel again if you have been conditioned to suppress your emotions and your feelings?

You do have feelings even if you have been taught to control them and keep them inside. To feel is a natural aspect of being human. You cannot stop it, but you can suppress it. What men need to do is stop suppressing their emotions and stop judging themselves for having them. It is important for men to let go of the artificial image of a "real man" and appreciate their natural sensitivity and vulnerability. Letting go of shame and judgment is the first step. Your heart always speaks to you. Respect that voice and realize that nothing is more powerful than the truth of the heart.

There are men who are sensitive and empathetic and have always chafed under the traditional ideal of tough masculinity. They empathize easily, absorb other people's suffering, and take on a lot of responsibility, which drains their energy and can make them sick.

This testifies to an excess of unbalanced feminine energy and a lack of self-awareness. This can occur in both men and women. If you suffer from this, it is important to focus your empathy on yourself and restore your boundaries by connecting with your own needs.

Men who connect easily with their feminine energy can clearly feel and express their feelings. Excessive giving and wanting to "save" the other, however, stems from a feeling of unworthiness, and not being allowed to stand up for oneself. Connecting to your heart as a sensitive man may mean that you become more self-aware and assertive. The connection with your heart restores the energetic balance between you and the other, and for some that means they become more tuned into their own needs and more respectful of their own boundaries. Others may need to open up more to the inner world of feelings, both in themselves and in others. The masculine heart energy, which I also referred to as the original or primordial male energy, is of significant importance in relationships, for men and women.

In the next chapter, I will talk in depth about the relevance of heart-based masculine energy to love, relations, and sexuality.

Chapter 9- Love, relationships, and sexuality

The original, heart-based masculine energy is an energy of discernment, responsibility, freedom, accepting one's individuality, and therefore, one's separateness. It can be viewed as a gift that wants to be developed. The higher masculine aspect of our soul enables us to understand and take on the role of separateness in relation to our own individuality. When we do this, we no longer look outside ourselves for security and validation.

Now let's talk about relationships.

Is the human desire for "true love" and to romantically merge with a partner a violation of one's individual autonomy? Is the urge to fall in love a sign of regressing to our helpless inner child who cannot tolerate feeling separate and disconnected, and reaches out to the "other" to provide security and love?

The higher masculine energy separates what needs to be separated, and sets boundaries where boundaries are proper and beneficial. There is still room for love, but only when there is no evidence of excessive craving, clinging and possessiveness, anymore. The excessive urge for unification is really a death drive that hinders the growth and maturation of your soul. This is why you feel suffocated when you adapt too much to someone else just to maintain harmony. You ignore your higher masculine energy's sense of self so you can continue to receive confirmation and warmth. It is of the utmost importance that people come to understand this desperate need for approval as a destructive desire that does not help them develop themselves, but rather stands in the way of true love. This applies to both men and women.

So, both women and men desperately need the original masculine energy to break free from addictive emotional dependence which causes you to sell yourself short just to gain another person's approval and affection?

This addictive dependence is an epidemic that plagues the whole of humanity and leads to dysfunctional, imbalanced relationships all around. It starts in your early childhood when you adjust to the expectations of your parents and other adults. During puberty, this compulsion to adapt and comply takes off even more.

While you are trying to free yourself from parental authority, its norms, and values, you face a new challenge, which is how to find your own identity in a social environment where peer pressure, the need to feel desirable, and have external success are the new standards to meet in order to be loved. Puberty is one of the most difficult stages in life, because you are forced to build an identity as a "male" or "female," while the images of masculinity and femininity presented to you are not heart-based at all. They are usually focused on external success, superficial, romanticized ideas about love and provide little insight into the real meaning of sexuality and relationships.

What is the real meaning of sexuality and relationships?

The real meaning or potential of a sexual relationship is for it to open the soul to a deep and powerful connection with another soul, one that goes beyond fixed images and expectations. It is a jump into the unknown, into the new, and into the part of yourself that wants to be seen and known. True love is guided by the principle of wanting to "receive the other person," to know them without judgement, to see them with the eyes of the heart. Sexuality guided by this heart-based intention can lead to love and a deep sense of connection that is not clingy or "blind." There will be challenges and issues, but the basic undertone of such a relationship is joyful and grounded.

Sexuality is a powerful energy that manifests itself in puberty as a raw desire for bodily union. This desire in raw form is not directed at the individuality of the other, but primarily at their physicality. It is not heart-based, yet it can be the start of something heart-based. The spiritual purpose of sexual attraction is to draw you to the potential for growth and love, as mentioned above, and it starts with an uncontrollable desire. You cannot suppress sexual desire; it's too overwhelming of a force for that. It cannot be controlled through the human mind, but it can be controlled through the human heart.

The flow of sexual desire draws two people together. When they grow close to each other an opening from heart to heart can arise, because as you give in to your sexual desires, you also get in touch with your deepest urge for unification and transcendence of your own self. The sexual drive within humans is never purely physical, even if it seems so. Because you are a conscious and emotional being, sexual contact with another cannot but touch a deeper layer within you, which holds the desire for contact on a soul level that is heart to heart.

In other words, sexuality is meant to be a gateway to the heart and to authentic human contact, but this is not what you are taught as an adolescent. In sex education more emphasis is placed on the biological aspects and yes, the emotional aspect is also addressed, but within a fairly stereotypical framework of "what men are like" and "what women are like." In the media, movies, and pop culture, young people are confronted with unrealistic, romanticized images of sex and love.

Not only is the true meaning of sexuality underrepresented and unexplained, but there is also a lack of relevant knowledge and understanding about the nature of love. Often the parents themselves do not know what a true love relationship is, and neither do the teachers. Sex education does not go any further than to warn and to give out information about the physical aspects. The emotional ups and downs that come with falling in love, the heartbreak, and sexual insecurities are barely addressed, because society as a whole doesn't know how to talk about them. Many taboos around sexuality have fallen away, but real freedom in this area is not so much about letting go of strict rules or dogmas, as it is about genuine communication and self-knowledge.

Sexuality opens up deep feelings, both fears and hopes, and to process them one has to understand the meaning of love relationships from the perspective of the soul. The soul is not interested in sugar coated visions of romantic bliss. It is far more interested in growing and expanding its awareness.

What do mainstream education and media tell you about that?

Taboos around sexuality have been relaxed, but many people still feel extremely lonely in their relationships and struggle to make sense of the images and ideals they were presented with when growing up.

The stakes are extremely high in the area of relationships. Love and sexuality affect all of us deeply and touch the essence of what we perceive to be the meaning of our lives. For example, I confess to having been very enamored of the idea of romantic bliss, the idea that falling in love meant merging with a loved one, a feeling of ecstasy that helps transcend the heaviness and loneliness of life.

Intellectually, I understand that I am an individual person, and that in relation to other people, I need to respect their boundaries as well as my own. But in reality, there has been a strong temptation to transcend all boundaries, especially when falling in love. I have observed in myself that the desire to merge with another, and feel completely one and safe, in the end creates a destructive dependence and the "death drive" you mention above.

Yet, I wonder if we can ever resist that temptation? Even when we understand from experience that it doesn't work, the desire is so strong that we fall prey to it every time. Are we really strong and autonomous enough to escape this?

In a world that is aggressive and indifferent, many people crave a sense of connection. The dominant masculine energy you see in society is one of control, struggle, competition, and coercion. As a young adult a lot is expected of you. You must be successful, sexually desirable, control your emotions, be positive and work hard, just to name a few expectations. You are not supposed to follow the flow of your soul if it deviates from these supposedly positive ideals. You are expected to comply with the existing order that is still in the grip of a fear-based masculine energy focused on control. Even in open and democratic societies, there are images and expectations at work that restrict you from following your heart.

The lack of heart-based awareness reinforces feelings of loneliness and meaninglessness in many people. There is a desire to "escape the world," and romantic love can be a way out of the feelings of despair and disconnection that many people experience.

However, if you hope to solve this existential pain through a relationship in which your authentic self is seen and loved, and be free of society's negativity, then you underestimate the extent to which "the world" is already inside you and your loved one. That's the real problem. What you dislike in the world—aggression, rudeness, indifference—is already within you, especially in the way you treat yourself.

Whether you are male or female, you have absorbed the competitive, controlling masculine energy that pervades society, and only by freeing yourself from it on the inside, can you free yourself from the world's pressures on the outside.

You are saying that the desire for an idealized romantic relationship is fueled by the dominance of a fear-based energy in society from which people seek to escape. We don't feel at home in this world, and that is another strong reason or impulse to look for "home" in a romantic relationship. But that's not the solution.

However, my question was, are we able to resist this temptation? I see that despair, loneliness, and loss are so great in our hearts that we still plunge back into, or can't break free from, imbalanced relationships that are based too much on emotional dependence or even addiction.

Yes, there are two options. Either you truly become aware of the real struggle going on inside you, or you continue to suffer and repeat dysfunctional relationship patterns. In essence, the choice is simple, you stop, or you continue.

What can help you stop is to consciously suffer. By that I mean you can observe your own feelings, behaviors, and thoughts in your interactions with people, your partner, and also your friends, family, and employer. By observing your inner reactions, you become aware of your own fears, the compulsion to fit in and do what others tell you to do. It shows you the extent to which you are silencing your own soul. The more you become aware of this, the more you start to sense your soul's presence, your most authentic thoughts, and feelings. Once you start to feel this living presence in your genuine inclinations in everyday life, you ignore it less and less. Your desire for freedom becomes greater than your desire for the approval of others. This is a birth process.

Does the desire for ideal love, for the ideal soul mate or "twin soul" then dwindle? Do you see this desire as an illusion?

Yes, to both. As the desire dwindles, you become more aware of what love really is, which is to accept and understand each other without forcing or draining the other to give you the approval and security you crave. Realize that the very idea of the ultimate and ideal partner is a high-strung notion that puts a lot of pressure on relationships. It is based more on a desire for love than on love itself.

Yes, that's an important difference.

Desire is a cry for light. Love brings light into the darkness.

Desire comes from darkness, the lack of something, and love comes from light, from abundance. Is desire actually pain?

Yes and no. Yes, it is painful because you feel that something is missing. When desire is willed, and is edged with fear, pain predominates. If the desire springs from a genuine need and comes from the soul, it gives joy, and feels positive, not painful. It feels like an opportunity or invitation. You are happily drawn to it. Instead of being impatient and tense about realizing your goal, you rely on your intuition and are attuned to the natural flow that leads to the fulfillment of desire.

The desire for a love relationship, for example, should be inspired by trust, otherwise there is always fear, impatience, contraction.

Yes, the desire must come from your soul.

And not from your ego or personality?

The ego is nothing but fear or contraction. It is not a separate entity. You don't have two selves, a lower one and a higher one, your ego and your soul. That's a false picture. You have one self—your soul. But parts of your soul are in a state of ignorance, fear, and separation. If your desire for a partner, a house, or a job originates from there, then what you will create or attract will not bring you what you expected.

Fear is not creative. You can generate a lot of energy using your willpower and fear to pursue your desires, but it will not bring you fulfilment and peace, even if you achieve your goals. For example, you form a relationship, find a nice house, and a respectable job, but in the end, it doesn't satisfy you as you anticipated it would. Something goes wrong, or you lose what you've just acquired, or you feel disappointed. Why? Because none of these things address the pain inside you. The fear and sense of lack that motivated you is still there.

To follow your soul's desire is to create out of a sense of abundance. You don't create or attract something in order to feel good and whole. It's the other way around, because you feel good and whole, you enjoy creating it. The creative process itself gives you joy and satisfaction.

Whatever you desire, check in with yourself and ask if the desire alone brings you joy.

To what extent do women cherish an idealized image of manhood and thereby reinforce the traditional, harmful, and narrow concept of masculinity?

I'm glad you asked because this gets to the heart of the issue. Women perpetuate the problem of the male wound when they continue to harbor false images of "what a real man is like," images that men cannot live up to. Women can hurt men by holding these expectations of them because men like to meet the expectations of women.

Sometimes these idealized images can influence a woman's psyche so strongly that she does not see who is really in front of her for a long time. In her interactions with her male partner, she does not see the unique man, but instead sees the one she hopes and expects to meet. At some point, cracks appear in that image—the man does not live up to her expectations. He has become human just like she is. The question then is whether there is still love between the two, can they let go of the ideal and communicate with each other as people.

Men also project their idealized image onto women. They too have unrealistic expectations. In both sexes, these expectations and tacit assumptions lurk in the background when choices are made to partner with someone. For example, a man seeks the sweet and gentle side of a woman, but turns away from her passionate, fiery side. He is unconsciously looking for his own feminine energy with which he is not sufficiently in touch, and then hopes to find it in his female partner, but he cannot entirely see or accept her as she is.

Is there such a thing as archetypal attraction or infatuation? By that I mean as a man you look for the ultimate feminine in a woman, and as a woman, vice versa. Does that mean you are more in love with an image than with the actual person?

This happens very often. If you have only limited contact with your soul, you may yearn to restore this connection, but if you do not know how, oftentimes, you will try to complete yourself through a sexual relationship. You try to make yourself whole be being with someone who radiates an energy that is opposite your own. It can be a difference in gender, the male-female polarity, but it can also happen in other ways. For example, one person is extroverted and exuberant, the other introverted and reserved; one is hypersensitive and empathetic, the other more down-to-earth and assertive.

Is this archetypal infatuation, and if so, what's the problem? Can't you develop yourself into a more complete person through this dynamic of opposites?

Yes, if there is a true connection on the soul level. Then the energy of attraction has a distinctive character, it is calmer in nature. Intense crushes that turn everything upside down are often a need or desire in a person that arises from a sense of lack rather than abundance. The attraction comes from an unconscious magnetism, an infatuation that absorbs you completely and may become obsessive.

Attraction that is felt on the soul level is accompanied by a feeling of joy. Joy is of the soul. Of course, someone with a contrasting character trait can inspire you. It is the essence of a love relationship that the unique form of the other person inspires you and deepens the relationship you have with yourself. But with an archetypal infatuation you fall in love with an image, for example, that of the strong man, the father, the protector, the teacher, or the strong mother-woman, the overwhelming seductress, the vulnerable child-woman who needs you.

The image is archetypal and in an immature relationship you desire the image more than the person. After a while, this leads to misunderstandings and to the conclusion that you do not know the other person and the other person does not know you. You are not struck by the soul energy of the other, but by the image you have formed of in which one quality or character trait is highlighted.

Your original goal to complete yourself through the other fails. You wanted to achieve this by becoming one with the other. That is what is wrong with this kind of magnetic and archetypal attraction, you are looking for a unity that is not possible for humans.

What about other creatures?

There are beings whose individuality is undeveloped, and for them, symbiosis or organic unity can be a very legitimate form of existence. Simply think of your hands attached to your arms. They cannot exist without your body, and they do not possess individuality in their own right. Your hands are of course unique, but they derive this uniqueness from your living body. On their own, cut loose from your body, they would be dead things. There is an organic unity between your hands and your animate body.

Can there be a symbiotic group consciousness in animals?

Yes, and it is appropriate there, because animals are unique in themselves, but they do not possess the kind of individuality found in humans.

Sometimes, I secretly wish for that kind of unity, to be absorbed in something greater, in the other, in something that releases you from your state of separation. I have always had that desire, and I see it in others as well.

Do human beings remember a symbiotic unity that we subconsciously long for? I am not thinking so much of the unity between mother and child in the womb, which is often not so idyllic, but rather of a group connection on a soul level that we experienced in the heavenly realms before this lifetime. I remember something like that, a deep connectedness in which you are still your unique self, but absolutely not as separate as you are on earth.

You cannot go back on your developmental path. The connection to which you refer actually still exists, but you are less aware of it during an earth life. When you channel, you sometimes feel it very strongly, and you feel uplifted. As a human being, you feel connected when you do something that inspires you. But when you sink back into a fear-based state of consciousness, you feel the separation again.

Then you start looking for that primal sense of connectedness in a relationship and become sensitive to archetypal crushes.

Yes, and then you are prone to the biggest mistake in this romantic man-woman story that your traditions have handed down to you—the belief that you are not whole and that you need another person, your "other half," to become whole and complete. See what's missing? The feeling of being one, in and of yourself, and rejoicing in the individual freedom that has been given to you.

The original masculine energy within you, whether you are female or male, puts you in touch with your unconditional freedom, your unique self, and frees you from that constant sense of lack, of "not being whole," that you experience. Your feminine energy enables you to connect, your masculine energy makes you aware of the one who connects—which is you. When you really feel that self, your unique soul, you no longer want to merge or dissolve into something bigger or someone different than yourself. You are the miracle born of Oneness, and at the same time a unique spark.

Relationships serve the purpose of helping you become more aware of yourself. They are not an easy fix for the hole you feel in your heart. If you expect that, you will be disillusioned. The rosy feelings collapse when you move beyond the attraction you had at the beginning when the idealized images you held were not yet confronted with everyday reality. Once you go deeper, you see the pain in the other, and realize you can't "fix" it. You have to understand this and understand that your partner is incapable of being your "ideal man or woman."

Is "the hole in the heart" about the fear of being alone?

Essentially, it is about the fear of being disconnected. This is the greatest fear. To feel the pain of separation—that is your specter. It's not about being physically alone. You can be alone and still feel connected, just like you can be with others and still feel separate.

That pain of separation has nothing to do with other people?

There is a metaphysical pain of separation that must be resolved on a metaphysical level. Simply put, there is an inner pain that cannot be taken away by anyone or anything outside of you. You need to resolve it by understanding and experiencing that you are part of the Whole, one with God or Source, and that you are not "becoming" Whole or One. The idea of "becoming" is a mistake. You don't have to work for connectedness and love, these are given to you.

In addition to the metaphysical pain of separation, there can also be human pain that arises from a lack of meaningful contact with others. You may have human contact that does not really nourish you. This is painful because as a human being it is natural for you to share your feelings and communicate with others.

What is a normal amount of contact? I find that confusing, because I like to be alone, and need it too, as many sensitive people do, yet I also have a strong need for meaningful communication. How does one know if that need is natural or if it arises from unprocessed metaphysical pain?

What matters with any contact you have is how it inspires you or invites you to express yourself. That is what determines the extent to which you feel fulfilled. There is a genuine need for communication between people, for friendship, sharing experiences, and supporting and encouraging one another. In other words, once you have overcome the inner pain of separation, you will still have a natural need to interact with other people. How much or how often is not fixed, it depends on your unique character and needs.

But what if that kind of contact is missing because people around you, even your family or partner, are unable to give it to you, for example, because of their emotional baggage? What to do if you don't meet enough like-minded people?

When you no longer struggle so much with the inner pain of separation, the metaphysical pain, then you will feel peaceful and self-confident. You won't take it personally if people do not understand you, even judge you, or drain you with their emotional sorrows. But you will start to meet people whose frequency resonates with yours, who are willing and eager to communicate with you from the heart.

It may also happen that you meet with a like-minded soul and there is a strong attraction and fascination, but after a relatively brief time it turns out that the connection creates too many emotional ups and downs. The feelings are intense, but the relationship cannot evolve in a steady, down-to-earth way.

I have two options in mind. You fall in love with someone who represents an archetype to you, for example, a father or mother figure. You fall in love with the image you have of the other more than with the unique person. In your fantasy, he or she is the father or mother you never had who you missed so much. The father who was warm and involved, the mother who was gentle and loving.

The second possibility is you fall in love with someone you know from a past life and with whom you had an intense and complicated relationship in which things were left unfinished. You feel a magnetic attraction to each other, compelling, sometimes obsessive, and it feels familiar and intimate. It feels like love. But if you go along with that flow, you soon encounter problems, confusion, conflict, and often it is impossible to be together for practical or emotional reasons.

Sometimes if those two possibilities go together then there is archetypal infatuation and karmic recognition. How should we regard this type of encounter?

This is not real love. What you describe as a compelling energetic pull or flow that tends towards the obsessive is a current that leads to an abyss rather than a grounded process of getting to know each other in depth. This latter process takes time and benefits from rest and relaxation, not urgency and obsession.

The energy of unresolved trauma is in that magnetic, coercive pull, but what brings you together is not mutual love, it is the strong urge of both souls to resolve unfinished business. However, everyone has to do this for themselves. In these types of relationships, there is often a need to let go of each other. There is something you need to solve for yourself, and you are challenged to do this through *meeting* the other, but you cannot do it *with* the other.

Genuine love is aimed at uncovering something new. Obsessive, archetypal, or karmic infatuation is aimed at uncovering something old that wants to be resolved.

That sounds clear on paper, but in practice it is difficult to draw the distinction properly because both feel like you're falling in love.

There is a big difference. Few people know what true love is. There may be real love in their life, but they can't recognize it. They are used to drama filled relationships. This is because they have never had a clear example of what constitutes a loving relationship.

In many relationships there is constant pushing and pulling. Unfulfilled promises are a source of tension and conflict in most relationships because spouses or lovers desire something from their partners that they cannot give. What is troubling them and responsible for the tension is what I call "the ideal of the Natural Beloved." Those who project this ideal believe in an illusion that is extremely persistent and brings drama and misunderstanding into their relationships. As long as you don't see through this, you cannot form a relationship based on love.

So true love is rare?

Yes.

What is this "ideal of the Natural Beloved?"

It is the idea that you "naturally" belong to someone, that there is someone who naturally fits and complements you and "makes you whole." This is a mistake. It is better to regard the other person as a mystery, as "unknown, but fascinating to get to know."

If you believe in the "Natural Beloved," you are not open to new experiences that love brings. You want to assimilate the other person and fit them into your framework of preconceived ideas. You want to fill up the hole inside you and do so by assuming a familiarity that is not yet warranted and appropriate.

There is magical thinking at work here—the desire to be fully known and understood. The belief in and desire for a "Natural Beloved" fulfills your fantasy. But this fantasy is childish and unreal. If you approach the other person with this fantasy in mind, your starting point is in fact selfish. You don't want to get to know the other person, you want the other person to fulfill your needs and you assume that he or she "naturally" has the right skills and qualities to do so. It's as if you think the other person already knows you.

When you put it that way, it's very shortsighted.

I put it a bit bluntly to help you become aware of a pitfall that causes many relationships to break down. It is indeed shortsighted. However, the important thing is to find out why you are doing it, how to notice it within yourself, and then release it.

Why are we doing this?

Because you do not know, love, and understand yourself enough. The longing to be known is an authentic longing. It underlies all spiritual growth. It is the soul's purpose to become more and more aware of itself.

The need for love, the longing to be known in a deep and compassionate way is a natural and spiritual desire in human beings. But because you have forgotten how to fulfill this need within yourself, and because your upbringing and education are too focused on gaining knowledge of the outside world, the natural desire for self-knowledge turns into a desire for the "Natural Beloved."

Yes, now I understand.

Be aware that the greatest challenge for you as a human being and a soul is to know all aspects of yourself. This is the way of the soul, the goal of the soul's journey through all its incarnations, and the journey never ends. It takes on ever richer forms of expression. It is a joyful path provided you consider yourself a special and delightful being to discover and understand. You should be in love with yourself. That is life's grand invitation. Meeting a loved one can awaken this rapture about yourself, about how special and unique you are, and stimulate your natural desire for spiritual growth. That is the meaning of love, and romantic love in particular.

Beautiful! How can we realize before it's too late, that we are projecting the ideal of the Natural Beloved on our relationship and thereby blocking or sabotaging a real exchange?

Idealization is counterproductive because you create tension when you do it. This tension comes from an expectation that idealization evokes. Expectation creates tension. That's the first thing that goes wrong.

Then there is the image behind the expectation. The content of the image may differ depending on your cultural background or age. But whatever the specific content is, the other must meet your idealized image of masculinity or femininity and that image is not based on what your soul wants, but what your personality finds desirable. These false expectations hurt the other because they ignore his or her unique truth or self, who they actually are with their own light and shadow parts. In addition, expectations create a tendency to judge the other, and thereby invoke the pain of rejection.

How do you notice whether you are projecting idealized or archetypical images on your relationship that cause tension and pain?

Take a look at your fantasies about the relationship. What is your ultimate fantasy or expectation of it? What does the other bring to you? What feeling does that evoke? If your fantasies are (very) compelling, pay attention. The quality of Love is not sweeping or grand or comes with great fanfare. Love is moving, enlightening, surprising, tender, confrontational, revealing. Love has to do with patience, being there for the other, not judging, and not so much wanting to make everything "better," but staying present with "what is."

Love is joyful, far removed from the madness you sometimes associate with being in love. It is not a scorching fire, but a soft flame that spreads its light silently. It is not a wild ecstasy, but a quiet knowing rooted in the present, illuminating both the past and the future.

Falling in love is exciting and refreshing, but you shouldn't glorify it. It is a game in which you break free from yourself, from your comfort zone, and experience and view yourself in a different way than you are used to. This can be extremely enriching, but if you make the other person too special, you lose your grip on reality and elevate the other person to a place of authority whose judgment makes or breaks you. Then you have become a slave. That is the opposite of being free and innovative.

First there is the excitement and anticipation of love and then there is the fear of losing it. What happens next?

You are not being true to yourself. The joy and self-development gained decrease as soon as you start taking the game too seriously and see the other person as the solution to your problems.

Does the original desire for real contact give way to a kind of childish desire for a solution that comes from the outside?

Yes.

Then you have the story or example of a woman who sees her father— who could not fulfill her childhood needs—in her lover, who finally fulfills it for her, or a man who sees the ideal mother he never had in real life in his lover.

Yes, that is possible.

Does this desire to merge with an uncritical other, and the urge to idealize also stem from the conditioning we have undergone as men and women?

Yes, of course. If you are taught when growing up as a girl to place the masculine energy outside of you, and when growing up as a boy to place the feminine energy outside of you, it is a breeding ground for intense, unrealistic desires for "the other half," and all the while the other half is already inside you.

As a man you have feminine energy, and as a woman you have masculine energy, both are part of your soul so they're already "yours." But someone else's energy is not "yours," and can therefore never complete you, nor is it meant to make you whole. Love relationships are meant to awaken you to your own potential, your own inner healing—not to lose your sense of self in an attempt to artificially become "one" with another.

This is a destructive desire, I understand. It is regressive instead of progressive, more like a childlike state, which feels limitless, the child still unaware of its own separate identity and boundaries. When we bring that energy into a relationship instead of the energy of well-defined adult boundaries it will create problems.

But there is also a strong sexual attraction between men and women, which leads to a kind of intoxication. Together with the myth of the Natural Beloved, it is a mix of physical and psychological attraction that is hard to resist. Or should one separate the sexual attraction from the childish desire for being healed and "made whole" by another?

Sexuality does not have to lead to intoxication. Sexuality can be light and pleasant, a delight to the senses and nurturing to the soul. But as soon as you project anything onto it, especially the childish desire for a fully present mother or father, a dependence can arise in one or both partners that is destructive. You make yourself vulnerable to rejection that hits hard, and that will inevitably happen, because the other person will never be the perfect partner of your dreams.

He or she is a human being with their own past, pain, and sensitivities, who may unconsciously project expectations onto you which you cannot fulfill. Often, it is an idealized image that you cannot live up to. It becomes impossible to meet their expectations and vice versa. The lightness goes out of the relationship, a heaviness remains that creates reproaches and misunderstandings and drives the partners apart.

To return to the notion that began this chapter, they no longer honor each other's freedom and individuality. When they project idealized images onto each other, the other is seen more as an archetypal figure instead of a living, unique person.

Indeed. This shows how the conditioning of a man, or a woman negatively impacts you. If you identify too strongly with being a man or a woman, instead of with your unique humanness, then you are always looking for the other half of yourself. Such a quest is an illusion. There is no other half, period.

It is precisely when you embrace your own wholeness as a unique soul that you pave the way for open, inspiring, and fulfilling connections with others, whether it is a sexual relationship, a professional one, or a friendship.

Part III- Four healing meditations

The following section consists of four channeled meditations on male energy that I received during a weekend workshop for men, which I held with trainer and coach Bouke de Boer. The channelings are primarily tailored to men, but their content is also relevant to women and the meditations are beneficial for them as well. If you do the meditations as a woman, you can connect with your own masculine energy, and imagine it taking the form of an inner boy or man.

Chapter 10- The original boy in you

I am Jeshua. I am speaking to you from a field of consciousness that is greater than all of us. As a soul, you are connected to a source of love and unity that is the origin of all life. Just feel it. Be present to it from your heart.

Being present from the heart is not self-evident. Male consciousness has been cast out of the heart. In the course of your childhood, you have all learned what it means to be a man. But as you grew up from boyhood to manhood certain parts of you were closed off, no longer accessible.

I invite you to connect with your body now. Your body is a field of energy, it is not a thing or a lump of matter. There is a huge amount of information stored in that field, which also includes solidified emotions and old ways of thinking. You are the consciousness that contains this field.

I invite you to connect with your body and take your awareness all the way into your heart. Then, sink your attention into your abdomen. Take a step back from everything around you, even the people who are close to you. Let go of all your thoughts and worries that may arise.

Take your attention to your core and feel it in your tailbone. There is a base point in your energy field at the very bottom of your spine. Focus your attention there and breathe into it. You are protected, you are safe. You are allowed to sink into yourself and distance yourself from everything outside of you. Feel how you need to rest within yourself. Become aware of your feet, and the ground beneath your feet. Feel the living earth below you and go even deeper within. This is your field, your inner space. This is yours! You are the consciousness that envelops this field. You are safe. Your consciousness is part of a meaningful Whole. You are not alone. You are connected.

Although you are connected to a part of a bigger Whole, you also need to stand on your own, to be the master of your own field. Your energy field is full of thoughts, feelings, hopes, pains, and desires. Your consciousness is not only equipped to hold and embrace this field, but also to transform it. You are here on earth in this life with a mission, an inner mission. That assignment is a secret, and discovering the secret of your mission is an adventure. There are no ready-made answers. You are an adventurer on your lifepath who discovers their own secrets. An important key to discovering your unique path, your secret, is to go inside yourself, back to the little boy you once were.

Inside you there is a boy who has not yet been touched by the influences of the outside world—the limiting thoughts and oppressive patterns that were imposed upon you as a child. There is the original boy who is free and still lives inside you. I invite you to connect to this boy. Maybe he is hiding. You all had to hide the original aspects of yourself, which were deemed too wild by those outside yourself for you to feel you fit in. Look for the rebellious part that you had to park on the sidelines, the anti-authoritarian part that did not want to comply with rules that seemed useless or unjust. You may experience this rebellious part indirectly in everyday life through feelings of dissatisfaction, irritation, or frustration. Often you don't realize where those feelings come from.

The original boy's sensitivity may also have been oppressed. Sensitivity, empathy, and compassion belong to your original masculine energy. The boy felt and perceived everything about his parents and other people close to him, and at some point, he was taught to restrain, suppress, and control his feelings. He had to cut off this part of himself, because it was not welcome—after all—a man is supposed to be strong, powerful, and in control.

I ask you to connect with your inner boy who is most eager to show himself to you now. Check if you can see a boy inside your inner space who completely belongs to you, who is part of your soul. Invite him to come closer and notice the expression on his face. What does he want to tell you? Is he stubborn and rebellious, is he poetic and creative, is he sad and lonely, or angry and mischievous? Greet him. He wants you to see and know him, because he is a very pure part of you that needs to be expressed.

Now ask that boy, "What bothers or weighs you down the most? How can I help you to freely express yourself?" Tell the boy you welcome him and that he no longer needs to hide. Give this boy a place somewhere in your energy field inside your body. Where does he want to be? In your heart? In your legs? In your stomach? He helps you to recognize and become aware of your soul's energy. He can be your guide once you no longer suppress him.

During this time of great chaos on earth, it is important that people, both men and women, restore contact with their original being, their soul. Instead of being determined by the past, let yourselves be guided by the new seeds that want to sprout and flourish. When you do your inner work, and discover and follow your own life path, you contribute to the greater whole. You are not doing this just for yourself. You are paving a path for others. You are a pioneer. Be proud of yourself! Trust yourself and honor your own courage.

Chapter 11- Making peace with the feminine energy

I am Jeshua. I speak from a unified field that surrounds all of you. I am connected to you as a soul, as a being that transcends your body. Your soul is present in this field beyond space, time, and matter and the field permeates you in the here and now. It has been called many names, love, consciousness, God, but in truth there are no words to describe it. It manifests itself as a field of tranquility and timelessness and it is possible for you to breathe and relax in it.

This field of consciousness is intimately interwoven with the reality of Earth and everything that happens there. You are part of this field and part of the transformation that Earth is going through. The consciousness of humanity is changing, driven by deep crises. People on Earth are suffering physically and mentally. Nature is also suffering. As a human being on earth, one of most profound things you suffer from is your sense of being cut off and disconnected. You seek connection with others, a partner, a friend, like-minded people, but at the same time, you are disconnected from your Self, from your own soul, and that hurts you the most.

When your whole being is in touch with this field by way of your soul, you feel warm and secure within. It is only when you are connected to this divine field of oneness that you feel anchored and at home wherever you are because Home is within.

I invite you to reconnect with your core essence, your soul. Turn your attention within and become aware of your body, of the tension in your muscles and the restlessness in your mind. By being consciously focused there for a short while, you can feel that the tension, anxiety, or pain is just one part of you, not all of you. You are more than that. You are bigger and vaster than anything that's bothering you right now.

Become aware of your body and consciously breathe into your abdomen. Feel the ground under your feet, it is the Earth who supports and carries you. You are not alone. The deeper you go within, the closer you get to the mystery of who you are. You are connected to all there is, inextricably linked to the whole of Creation, and yet you are unique. There is no one like you. You have walked your own path, your light sparkles in a way that is uniquely yours like a fingerprint. Your unique divinity is the most precious gift you have and the most precious gift you give to others. It is your mission to discover your light, your soul's unique radiance. To know and express your Self will bring you the highest joy imaginable.

Today, we are talking about masculinity and masculine energy. Simply ask yourself this—is my masculine energy a channel for my soul or does it block the outflow of my unique soul's energy? The soul's energy flows out of you through your earthly personality, energy field, and body. The meditation in the previous chapter was about the boy in you, the boy who is still free from outside influences, who is connected with your true self.

Look at how your parents modeled masculine and feminine energy. Your father or someone who filled in for him functioned as your first role model for how to express male energy. Go back to being the young, pure boy again who is inside you—free and uninhibited—and look at your father through his eyes. Focus on feeling your father's energy and how it affected you emotionally. Sense whether he suffered from being a male. Did he have to restrict himself because of outside expectations and obligations? Feel his pain and inner struggle but stay outside of it. Look at it, but realize it is not your job to fix it. It is not your struggle. It never was and it isn't now. What informed him about how to be masculine and what did he pass on to you? What prevented him from being himself, from expressing himself? See how that affected you. What masculine imprint did he leave on you?

Now go into your heart area and feel it in an energetic way. The center of the original boy's heart is open, allowing the feminine and masculine energies to be equally present. The feminine aspect of the heart is about connection, empathy and reaching out to others. The masculine aspect has to do with self-awareness, clarity, setting boundaries and taking care of yourself. The masculine heart energy is characterized by its ability to focus and discern. Were those qualities modeled by your father when you were growing up, or did you have to adjust to his rules and expectations? In other words, expectations of an external authority figure. What happened to your masculine energy as you were growing up?

Men carry a collective psychological burden inside. Historically, men were taught to shut down their feelings. Their responsibility was to protect others. As head of the family, they were expected to be leaders. If war broke out, they would have to leave home and go fight to defend their country. Men worked to provide for their family, and when called up, went to war as a solder.

In situations like these, men had to close off their feelings at least partially. To follow an outside authority—employer, boss, politician, army leader—you had to be obedient while suppressing your own sense of truth and creativity. While the original masculine energy of the heart is about self-awareness and standing up for your true self, there is a collective heritage instilled in men that demanded they be disciplined and suppress their feelings. They were taught to fit into society and be "good responsible men," who served the interests of family, company, and country.

This psychological burden they had to carry severed their connection to their original fire and aspirations to connect with heart-based masculine energy. This is how a semblance of the "good man" was created. The good, ideal man was a disciplined worker, a follower serving various worldly authorities outside of him, and furthermore, a man who could control his emotions and shut down his heart. This expectation to always perform as the "ideal man" restricted and imprisoned men, especially sensitive men, and forced them into a box where their soul withered, and their life's energy was drained out of them.

Behind this mask they were forced to wear, anger, bitterness, and resentment eventually piled up. They might be aware of being angry and frustrated, but it was harder to get in touch with the underlying pain of having to constantly deny yourself, much less the sadness of being disconnected from your heart and intuition. Precisely because it was forbidden for men to be weak or vulnerable, it made it easier for them to feel angry and frustrated rather than feel the pain and sadness underneath it. Yet, it is vitally important for men to be in touch with this wound. When you open your heart to yourself and face the suffering you find there, you reconnect with your higher masculine energy.

Opening your heart is also the way to allow your feminine energy back into your awareness. As a human being and as a soul, you carry both male and female energies inside, and you need both. It is unhealthy to suppress one and completely identify with the other.

I invite you to connect with your feminine energy in your imagination and see her as a woman on a stage. You might call her your "inner woman" who represents the feminine part of your soul and brings you back in touch with your feelings and sensitivity. Your inner woman is in direct contact with your heart-based masculine energy. On the heart level, the masculine and the feminine belong together. Look into the eyes of this woman and feel her energy just as you did with the young boy. Ask her to come out of her hiding place and show herself to you. Welcome her. Feel the spark of recognition and familiarity. She is a part of you and lives inside your heart.

Closely observe her appearance. Is she happy and peaceful, or lonely and distraught? At first, you may feel uncomfortable with her. You could have been negatively influenced by the kind of femininity presented to you in the past either by your mother or other female role models in your life. You can let that go now and allow this unique feminine energy before you to spontaneously present itself in a way that is more befitting.

This feminine part of you wants to tell you something. It wants to be seen and integrated into you again. She carries an intuitive wisdom that had to be suppressed. It is *your* intuition. Let her tell you through a word, a gesture, or a feeling what is important for you to know at this time in your life. Make peace with her.

If for some reason you have difficulty allowing the feminine energy in, use your imagination to perceive her as a little girl so you can feel her light and innocence. It is possible that your hesitation to embrace feminine energy is because you have felt threatened by it in your past relationships with women and as a result, find it difficult to connect with your own feminine side. When you experience this feminine energy as a girl, it will be easier for you to connect with her. Take this little girl by the hand, take her into your heart and hold her.

The original masculine and feminine energies are not in conflict with each other. They are meant to complement and support each other. Let the boy you have met before join together with the girl and imagine them both inside your heart now. They are reaching out to each other and enjoying each other's company. Allow this genuine reunion of the masculine and feminine to take place inside you. Own your feminine energy, and you will be a free man.

Chapter 12- Welcome your original masculine energy

I am Jeshua. I speak to you from a field of togetherness, a field of light and unity that connects us as souls.

What is the soul, really? It seems like a mystery, unfathomable. The soul is the source of life. Your soul has chosen the life you are in now, a life on earth, a life as a man or a woman. Your soul is thirsty for experience, it wants to live life fully. The soul does not judge in terms of right or wrong and does not avoid the pain life can bring. It wants to experience the heights and depths, and thereby gain knowledge about life on earth.

Be in touch with and feel your own consciousness, it is a living field. There is a consciousness within you that observes without judgment, ever fresh, alert, and open. Be aware of it on the physical level. Imagine that all the cells of your body from top to bottom are infused with this lively awareness. You are a living field of consciousness. Sink deeper into yourself now, and focus your attention on your chest, your heart. Let your mind be as neutral as possible. You don't need anything. Just breathe and be. Enjoy the silence. As you sink into this space, you experience how vast your consciousness is. You are old and wise; much wiser than you think.

In everyday life, you are preoccupied with your worries and emotions, bogged down by old patterns of thinking and feeling. But your consciousness intuitively knows the purpose of your life. Breathe into your abdomen, your tailbone or root chakra, and let your consciousness flow into your legs and your feet. Feel how welcome you are on earth. Your soul, your consciousness wants to be here. There is a "Way" for you here, but to find it, you must first accept that you are where you are. Your soul does not judge that. At times, you think you've gone off track, have failed to "fulfill your mission," but your soul does not see it that way. Your soul wants to explore everything and finds all human experience valuable.

Every one of you shares a deep longing for wholeness, and many of you seek it, along with the desire to feel at Home in a love relationship. But precisely because your expectations are high and your desires strong, relationships are where you may experience the deepest suffering.

Connect with your masculine energy now and feel it flow through your body. Stay neutral, feel at ease, open, and curious. Connect to the instinctive part of your male body. To help you do this, imagine there is an animal beside you who represents this instinctive aspect. Invite the animal to come close to you. Welcome it. Feel its wildness, how it wants to be free. Sense what this animal needs. What does it say to you?

The soul has a masculine and a feminine side. Without both of these energies you could not even be incarnated as a human being. You need both. But if you have been born into a male body and have experienced what it is like to be a man, you've been confronted with images, rules, and values to live up to, which have been superimposed on you. In many traditions, especially religious ones, the original instinctive energy was considered sinful, suspicious, and "out of control." The higher masculine energy is instinctively strong and wants to face the Truth. However, in fear-based cultures and traditions, men were forced to suppress not just their feminine, feeling side, but also their original masculine energy.

Allow the forbidden male to speak. If you befriend the animal beside you, connect to its strong instinctive power, what would be the first thing you would do? What would you do differently? What would you change? Dare yourself to be in touch with it. Allow the animal's energy to fill your body from the tips of your fingers down into your toes. Feel this animal's power, its wisdom, its instinctive power. Own this energy. At the same time, be aware of your consciousness as an open, neutral field of awareness.

You are welcome on earth. Your soul chooses to be here. You have something important to contribute. You are here to experience and express yourself. When you do, you pave the way for collective consciousness to change and open up to the truth. Human beings hold repressed energies within them that cause pain, suffocation, and suffering. Both the masculine and feminine energies carry deep emotionally charged blueprints that dictate how to be and act. These blueprints are passed on from generation to generation. As a son, possibly a father, you stand in a long generational line. How do you contribute something positive to the collective energy of mankind? One way is to free yourself from these pre-existing blueprints, these mental boxes you have been put in, the inherited pain, and repressed energy that is handed down to you from your family.

You have to liberate yourself first. You cannot free anyone else but yourself. You and only you can choose to break free, but you cannot make that choice for another even though you would like to prevent their suffering. When you free yourself, a spark of illumination is sent down your entire family line, to generations before you and after you, to the past and to the future. It is not a matter of willpower to liberate yourself from the repression and suffocation of these past blueprints. It is a matter of going within and welcoming yourself.

You can be who you are.

Heart-based masculinity is welcome on earth. It is time to step out of prison. Listen to the animal within you who knows how to sense energy in a pure, direct way. Your heart-based or original masculine energy is attuned to freedom, creativity, and independence. In this time of momentous change and transition, the return of heart-based masculinity is of significant importance. The awakening of consciousness is not just about allowing the original feminine energy back and reconnecting with it. It is just as much about reconnecting with the original masculine energy.

The effects of ego and fear-based masculine energy are clearly visible in the way authoritarian political leaders rule and create conflicts, in the way nature and mother earth are exploited. It is time for the masculine energy to rise beyond its ego phase and embrace the next stage of evolution. You are forerunners. You are in the process of letting go of the past and embracing a new type of masculine energy. That is your contribution to the collective, to shoot holes in mainstream consciousness and become an example of the new.

You are still seekers exploring unfamiliar territory. At times you wander around in circles and feel lost and lonely.

That is okay. Let it be.

You are welcome on earth.

It is your sincerity, honesty and vulnerability that will lead you to the truth.

The New Earth awaits you.

Chapter 13- Healing the collective male wound

I am Jeshua. We stand in a field of shared energy. Each one of you has emotions and thoughts that seem personal, and yet they are not. You all share a history and have been influenced by the collective energy field of humanity. During this time of global crisis, there is a dire need for transformation and change. There is a great deal of pain and suffering in the world, and a deep loneliness in people's hearts. You are not here just for your own self. A light wants to manifest through you that offers the way out of mainstream, fear-based consciousness.

If you looked at the earth and humanity from the outside, you would perceive a gray fog surrounding their collective energy fields. This is an indicator that people are surrounded and affected by a dense layer of fear that cuts them off from love, and other people. Fear suffocates and shuts people down, affecting any understanding of their true purpose. It robs them of meaning in their lives. Those of you on a spiritual path are in your own way becoming aware of how fear holds you back and how to overcome it.

Within the collective energy field surrounding the Earth, the light of truth and transformation is being lit everywhere on the planet. This light always emanates from within. Real change will come to Earth not from above, but from below. It is birthed through individuals who honestly examine their own darkness and confusion, and who feel an urgent desire to be free of it. They are the real leaders at this time.

Those in positions of worldly power are completely caught up in the dense fog. Change will rather come from people who "drop out," who distance themselves from mainstream consciousness, who dare to be different. You belong to that group of invisible pioneers. You cannot fit into the energy of the past. You are unable to ignore the call from the future, the call for a different type of consciousness, more open, more honest, more in touch with the heart, more deeply connected with one's true self and the true selves of others.

I invite you to connect with that part of you who is the pioneer, the invisible leader, the teacher, and turn your attention to the issue of the masculine energy, the male wound. Imagine that you see the energy field of the "average man" in front of you, who feels stuck, unable to feel his feelings, express his creativity and break free, and is inwardly crying out for release.

When you look at this man's energy field, which is the result of centuries of brainwashing, can you specifically locate any dark areas indicating tension and pressure in his body? His heart is strained from suffering emotional pain, but at the same time he suppresses it, because he is not allowed to feel it. He feels restless and on edge. He hides his sensitivity, feels he has to be strong and decisive, and all the while he has a hole in his heart.

Look at what happens inside him. In order to survive, he hides his vulnerability, and focuses his effort on thinking. He withdraws into his head, but it does not solve anything, it does not diffuse the enormous tension he holds inside—to have feelings, but not be allowed to express them.

Feel the uneasiness and frustration in this man. He is like a caged tiger. He wants to break out of prison because he feels he could explode, but anger and aggression do not help him find a way out. Unconscious anger and frustration only alienate him from people and from his own sensitive nature, his heart. The most unconscious and therefore darkest place in his masculine energy is trapped in the repetitive survival mechanism of thinking too much, working too hard, and trying to be a "good, strong man."

The repetitive survival mechanisms of overthinking, overworking, and trying to be a "good, strong man," are the most unconscious and darkest aspects of his masculine energy. That is where he feels trapped. He is not in touch empathically and suppresses his creativity and intuition to be obedient to outside authorities while an undercurrent of constant fear and rage eats away at him. This is what makes up the energy field of "the average man," this is what it looks like. What part do you play in relation to this collective pattern, this collective male shadow? You have partially stepped out of that prison already, otherwise you wouldn't be reading this book.

Feel deep within to what extent you are out of this prison. How free is your heart? Then turn your attention to this "average man." Are you willing to be in touch with him? To do so, imagine him sitting on the ground in a cage, entrapped by bars. He wants to break out but has no idea how. What would you like to say to him?

Imagine walking up to him and finding a way to create a door to his prison. Invite him to open the door. What happens? You may see aspects of your father, your grandfather, and male ancestors going back many generations within this imprisoned man. Think of yourself as a liberator. Reach out to the man in the cage and take his hand.

Part of you is still inside that prison, but another part is outside it. Clearly feel this. Feel your wisdom, your compassion, both for yourself and for all men. What does the caged man need the most? You can send it to him energetically. It can be done without words, simply by being there and feeling the compassion you have for him in your heart.

You have suffered in your own way from living up to other people's expectations of how to be masculine. Perhaps you suffered from an absent or aggressive father or did not receive sufficient attention and emotional nourishment as a boy. Yet, you stand here with love and wisdom in your heart. You are the sons of this history and at the same time the fathers of a new generation. Even if you are not a father biologically, you are a father energetically, to everyone who comes after you.

What makes you a pioneer and leader is not primarily determined by what you do or manifest in the outside world. It is first and foremost an inner feat—daring to be different, willing to explore the depths of your feelings, facing the darkness within. Your role as a spiritual pioneer is exemplified by what you radiate out to others, how you touch people with a look, a gesture, a way of being. A living example is worth more than a thousand scholarly words. Theory and dogma are mere secondhand knowledge, which bear little weight by comparison.

Being a teacher in essence is about transmitting energy, and resolution is the energy that you have awakened and transformed inside yourself, and shine onto others. It is a vibration that people pick up on flawlessly, even if you do not intend to "heal them."

The light of your soul will attract whatever you need and find its course naturally without willful effort.

Have faith in your light.

Don't worry about outward achievements and success.

Succumb to the power of your inner light.

Acknowledgments

I would like to thank a number of people for their help in the creation of this book. First of all, as with all my previous books, I have felt strongly supported and stimulated by the inspiring conversations with Gerrit Gielen.

I am grateful to Bouke de Boer for organizing and jointly offering a special weekend workshop for men, the meditations from which are included in part III of the book. I am grateful to the workshop participants, as well as to a number of male readers whom I later interviewed for this book, for their openness and trust.

Much gratitude to Suzy Conway for her meticulous editorial work on the English edition.

About the author

Pamela Kribbe (based in The Netherlands) holds a PhD in philosophy and has been working as a writer and spiritual therapist since 2002. Her books, notably *The Jeshua Channelings, Heart Centered Living, The Christ Within and The Forbidden Female Speaks,* focus on the transition from ego to heart-based consciousness and have been published in several languages. She offers workshops and lectures in the field of inner growth and emotional healing, often in collaboration with hypnotherapist Gerrit Gielen.

More information about them and their work can be found on their website—www.jeshua.net.

Other books by Pamela Kribbe

The Jeshua Channelings

In clear and accessible language, Jeshua speaks about the origins and destiny of the lightworker family. He offers a detailed account of the transition from ego-based to heart-based consciousness. In the second part of the book, Jeshua deals with several aspects of everyday life, such as relationships, work and health. He addresses the most common questions and problems we struggle with in these areas.

Some books are filled with shining wisdom. Others radiate great love. A few – a very rare few – are overflowing with both. The Jeshua Channelings is one such book. If you want to know who you really are, why you're here, and what your life is truly about, look no further. This book gently and compassionately guides readers toward remembering their magnificence as divine souls. Brilliantly insightful and inspiring, it is true gem and a blessing to our world.

- Robert Schwartz, author, Your Soul's Plan: Discovering the Real Meaning of the Life You Planned Before You Were Born - yoursoulsplan.com

ISBN-13: 978-1601456823
Paperback: 264 pages
Publisher: Booklocker.com, Inc.

Heart Centered Living

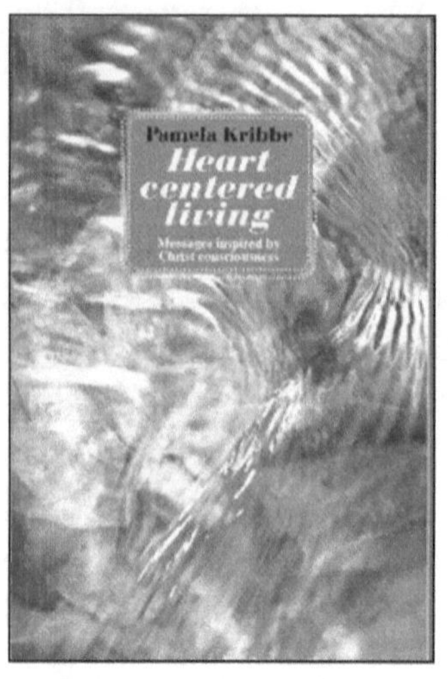

Heart Centered Living is living according to the calling of your soul. You can recognize the calling of your soul by the feelings of joy, peace and inspiration it brings to you. However, daring to trust your heart often involves a leap into the unknown. You may be confronted with deep-seated fears about your own worth and your ability to pursue your own path. This book is a loving guide on your way to heart centered living. It contains clear and informative channelings inspired by the Christ energy. They deal with different subjects, such as finding your true passion, how to create balanced relationships, parenting the new, sensitive children and emotional healing in the face of fear and depression. They also speak about the profound transformation humanity is going through, letting go of ego-based consciousness and evolving into heart-based consciousness.

This book is written for lightworkers, souls who feel compelled to go deep within and express their true soul's calling on Earth. The teachers who speak in this book (Jeshua, Mary and mother Earth) all encourage you to take the leap of faith and become who you really are. Their teachings gently inspire you to face and overcome whatever holds you back in listening to the voice of your heart.

ISBN-13: 978-1621412618
Paperback: 276 pages
Publisher: Booklocker.com, Inc.

The Christt Within

In each of us, Christ consciousness is waiting to be awakened. Christ consciousness is the awareness that behind outer appearance and form, all life is one and connected. As we enter this level of awareness, we gradually let go of our fear, our resistance, our need to control. We discover the reality of our divine essence, our soul. Life becomes less about struggling to survive, driven by the demands of the ego, and more about joy and creating from the heart.

Opening up to the voice of our soul involves taking a leap into the abyss: you are invited to rely on your inner guidance rather than the outer directions you are used to steering by. How do you let go of the worldly pressures and judgments that have become almost second nature? How do you know if you have truly connected with your soul? How do you deal with fear and trauma, which keeps you from surrendering?

The spiritual messages in this book, received by way of channeling, are meant to answer these questions and to assist you on your path of inner transformation in a loving and compassionate way. As you surrender to your soul, the Christ Within will awaken and illuminate your life as well as the lives of others.

ISBN-13: 978-1626469631
Paperback: 264 pages
Publisher: Booklocker.com, Inc.

Dark Night of the Soul

This book contains Pamela's personal story of the deepest crisis she ever experienced in her life. Successful as a writer and spiritual therapist, she was confronted first with illness, then with insomnia and fear, and ultimately with depression and psychosis. She had to be hospitalized and undergo psychiatric treatment. Pamela openly describes what she went through and also seeks to come to terms with what happened to her from a spiritual perspective. What do depression and psychosis mean from the perspective of the soul? How do they arise and can they bear fruit? What is the role of psychiatry in a dark night of the soul?

The second part of the book contains a series of channeled messages about the meaning of severe crises in our lives, the need to face our own darkness, and the unfailing presence of love and compassion in our lives.

ISBN-13: 978-1634908788
Paperback: 248 pages
Publisher: Booklocker.com, Inc.

The Forbidden Female Speaks

Mary Magdalene was regarded as "the forbidden female" in the Christian tradition: wild, free and sinful. This book contains a dialogue with and messages from Mary Magdalene, channeled by Pamela Kribbe (PhD). It is about male and female energy, relationships, sexuality and healing. In these teachings, Mary Magdalene speaks with a clear, loving voice that is sometimes direct and confrontational but mostly compassionate and deeply appreciative of human nature.

In both men and women, there is a forbidden female energy, Mary Magdalene says, which has to do with feeling, intuition and the heart. In this day and age, both sexes are invited to become aware of this energy and to heal the old wound of separation between them. In this way, we will learn how to listen to our heart's whispers again and reconnect with our soul.

ISBN-13: 978-1632637048
Paperback: 200 pages
Publisher: Booklocker.com, Inc.

Earth Speaks
Messages from Mother Earth

Have you ever considered the possibility that Earth is alive and has a consciousness of her own? If so, wouldn't you want to know what Earth has to tell us about who she is and about who we are? In this book you will find messages from Earth, which Pamela Kribbe has received through channeling. Earth speaks about the living consciousness that is present in plants and animals and invites people to reconnect with nature. Above all, she beckons us to come home to our own nature. By thinking and controlling less, and trusting our original, feeling nature, we will create more joy and balance in our lives.

ISBN-13: 978-1647192600
Paperback: 114 pages
Publisher: Booklocker.com, Inc.

www.ingramcontent.com/pod-product-compliance
Lightning Source LLC
Chambersburg PA
CBHW051456250726
48655CB00001B/436